M000307067

I have known Jerry and Denise for the better part of ... academics-turned-well-trained-counselors know suffering hearts and the heart of God like few others. In *The Missing Commandment: Love Yourself,* they place emotional and spiritual health on a solid foundation of love—for God, for others, and for self.

—Gary W. Moon, MDiv, PhD, executive director, Dallas Willard Center for
Christian Spiritual Formation; author, *Apprenticeship with Jesus*

Jerry and Denise Basel are living out in a profound way what a growing movement of authors, songwriters, theologians, and everyday people have been daring to express, believe, and try on. It is the Original Good News, aimed at the lies we've been telling ourselves about us. The Basels display with winsome confidence the astonishing love of the Father; which alone allows us to love ourselves honestly, deeply and wonderfully.

—John Lynch, Bruce McNicol, and Bill Thrall,
bestselling coauthors, *The Cure, Bo's Cafe,* and *The Ascent*

Jerry and Denise brilliantly uncover the issues that are hiding in the dark corners of our story. This book will give you permission to love yourself the way God loves you. Though it may feel selfish, it's the most unselfish thing you can do.

—Pattie Mallette, New York Times bestselling author, *Nowhere but Up*

When you read *The Missing Commandment: Love Yourself,* you need to be ready for open-heart surgery. As I read it, I felt the invisible hands of grace soothe the pain and numbness out of my heart. If you want to live from the whole of your heart and feel Jesus living through and in you, then this book is a must.

—Pablo Giacopelli, professional tennis coach on the WTA Tour;
author, *Holding On Loosely.*

Whenever I have a chance to review a book, I ask myself, "Would I use this material in my ministry?" In the case of this book the answer is, absolutely. I believe God is going to use the message of this book to set many people free.

—Ken Nash, teaching pastor, Cornerstone Church, Grand Rapids, Michigan

The message of the Father's love is incredibly important in this hour. Jerry and Denise Basel carry a clear anointing to minister this message to the hurting and broken. They possess a keen awareness of the need for ministry in this area, not only because they have extensive counseling and teaching experience but also because they themselves live close to the heart of God.

—Billy Humphrey, director, International House of Prayer Atlanta;
author, *To Know Him*

I am pleasantly surprised at the simplicity yet power of Jerry and Denise Basel's book, *The Missing Commandment: Love Yourself.* It is not a typical Christian "advice book," but rather, a truthful, profound, and appropriate treatment of a fundamental issue affecting all of our lives. You will find real truth and healing in its pages. Be warned—it can change your life!

—Rev. Alfred Ells, MC, executive director, Leaders That Last Ministries;
counselor; consultant; author, *One- Way Relationships* and *Leaders That Last*

Written from the compassionate view of seasoned counselors, Jerry and Denise carefully guide us through the various issues of life and into the Father's waiting arms. Filled with precise biblical insight, poignant testimonies, professional counsel, and practical exercises, this is indeed a rich read.

—Ed Piorek, Father Loves You Ministries; speaker;
author, *Father Loves You* and *The Central Event*

The Missing Commandment: Love Yourself is a must-read for every person interested in going deeper into the intimate and personal love that our heavenly Father has for us. To love ourselves in a healthy way is simply coming into agreement with how God already loves us. Jerry and Denise have done an amazing job of communicating this simple yet profound truth.

—Barry Adams, Father Heart Communications; speaker; author, *Father's Love Letter*

In *The Missing Commandment: Love Yourself*, Jerry and Denise take you on a heart expedition that will help you discover who you really are—the glorious person God has created you to be and whom he truly loves.

—Gary Barkalow, founder, The Noble Heart;
author, *It's Your Call: What Are You Doing Here?*

This book is not just information: it is a guided path to healing, restoration, wholeness, forgiveness of self, and freedom from shame. The Basels write with simplicity, using narrative and grace-filled Scripture grounded in their personal experiences and the testimonies of others. This work is a must for every pastor and counselor and for individuals searching for a solid path to freedom from the wounds and lies that have ensnared them. It will surely be a companion to me as I reflect on my own journey and counsel others.

—Tom Colwell, director of pastoral care, Credential Holders and Pastors, Pentecostal Assemblies of Canada, Western Ontario District; co-founder, Men of Life Ministries, Canada

I am so excited about this book that words fail me. I don't think I've read anything like it: personal and didactic at the same time in a very easy flow. I felt like I was sitting in the counseling room talking to Jerry and Denise. Their easy style of talking yet getting to the heart of the matter came through so well. I thought of my clients in the addiction center and I can see it transforming lives. I can't wait for it to come out because I'll buy it in bulk.

—Dr. Bill Curnow, L.I.F.E. Coaching International, Wyoming, Michigan

Jerry and Denise have written a powerful book. Reading it caused me to become more vulnerable than I had imagined. It challenged me to consider whether I truly love myself as God calls me to. This book is full of poignant illustrations from real people and real experiences, and of practical and thought-provoking wisdom from two skilled counselors. These pages graciously invite the reader to discover and practice self-love and to truly understand, embrace, and rest in the love of God the Father.

—A. J. Gregory, author, *Messy Faith* and *Silent Savior*; writer/collaborator, *Nowhere but Up* with Pattie Mallette

Finally I have a single, solid book to give clients which can help them get to the real issue under the issues. We all need to know the Father's deep love for us experientially in order to be free to be who he made us to be—able to love and live fully because our hearts are fully convinced we are lovable, worthy, valuable human beings. I heartily recommend this book.

—Lorraine Turbyfill, M.Ed., licensed professional counselor; certified sex therapist

The Missing Commandment: Love Yourself is a gem for every follower of Christ, especially those called to assist others on the road to inner healing. Jerry and Denise have carefully articulated the Father's heart on the issue of loving ourselves. If you're a pastor, you should read this book for personal reflection and deeper discovery of God's amazing grace. This book will also become a powerful tool in the hands of your church members as they, too, seek to love what God loves—themselves. Your church will have a greater measure of God's love to offer a hurting, broken, and lost world.

—Greg Mayo, senior pastor, Cornerstone Church of Augusta

The Missing Commandment: Love Yourself is a must-read in our search for true healing in intimacy with others and with God. Jerry and Denise have captured the heartbeat of this crucial struggle and provided biblical direction. Through life stories and scriptural truth, they weave a beautiful message of hope and healing. For those who long to be awakened to their true identity in Christ, this book will clearly lead readers toward finding peace and wholeness in him.

—Kimberly Powers, co-founder, Walk the Talk Youth Ministries, Inc.; speaker; author, *Escaping the Vampire: Desperate for the Immortal Hero*

This book touches the deep places of the heart, filling in a missing piece of spiritual formation that has largely been neglected by the church. The Basels direct us toward Father God, helping us see ourselves as he sees us. With grace and truth, they show us the way to experience inner healing and to understand the Father's heart toward us. If you seek a resource to help you experience the Father's love in a deep and fresh way—then this is it!

—Rick Mailloux, lead pastor, Pequea Brethren in Christ Church, Lancaster, Pennsylvania

One of the great hindrances to people's receiving the Father's love is their inability to see themselves as he sees them. Jerry and Denise do a masterful job of helping readers find a pathway of healing from the self-hatred and low self-esteem that many have embraced for a lifetime. *The Missing Commandment: Love Yourself* must not be ignored.

—Roger and Gerri Taylor, co-founders, Places In The Father's Heart, Inc.; coauthors, *Our Glory Stories* and *The Heart of Marriage*

THE MISSING
COMMANDMENT
LOVE
YOURSELF

It's not missing from the Bible. It's missing from our lives.

THE MISSING COMMANDMENT
LOVE YOURSELF

HOW LOVING YOURSELF THE WAY GOD DOES
CAN BRING HEALING AND FREEDOM
TO YOUR LIFE

JERRY AND DENISE BASEL

HEART & LIFE
PUBLISHERS

In memory of
Shelley Byers
1971-2012
Our spiritual daughter,
Special friend and greatest cheerleader.
You only got to read the first two chapters of this book,
And even with only that, you were ready to give a copy
to everyone you knew.
Shelley, we will see you again someday, and what a day that will be.
SERIOUSLY!
Until then, you will always live fully alive in our hearts.
We love you and miss you so much.

The Missing Commandment: Love Yourself

Copyright © 2013 by Jerry and Denise Basel
All rights reserved.

Published in Grand Rapids, Michigan by Heart & Life Publishers, a division of Miles Media, LLC. www.heartandlife.com

ISBN 13: 978-0-9839924-8-6
Ebook ISBN: 978-0-9839924-9-3

Unless otherwise noted, Scripture quotations are from The Holy Bible, New International Version®. Copyright © 1973, 1978, 1984, 2011 by Biblica, Inc™. Used by permission of Zondervan. All rights reserved worldwide. www.zondervan.com.

Editor: Bob Hartig
Cover design: jeffgiffordcreative.com
Author photo: Christa Wilson, Raebeam Photography
Interior design: Frank Gutbrod

Unless specifically noted by the authors, names, dates, locations, and other details have been purposely changed to protect the identities and privacy of those discussed in the book.

Printed in the United States of America

THE MISSING COMMANDMENT: LOVE YOURSELF

INTRODUCTION

This book is about the heart—your heart and ours. From the very beginning of our ministry, God made it clear that the heart was to be central in everything we did. As I (Jerry) went through an intense, two-year period of emotional healing many years ago, I became aware that there were many things about the heart—my heart and God's heart—that I didn't understand. During this period, I became very aware of how my heart had been affected by childhood wounding, and I came to understand that God had a plan to restore and heal my heart.

Denise and I were university professors at the time, and God began to share that the healing of my heart would also involve a significant change in my personal calling and destiny. Walking into a church service one Sunday, I could "see" and feel the emotional condition of those around me. Although the majority of the people looked fine and together on the outside, I sensed that many were really hurting on the inside. They were each wearing masks that covered their true conditions, and I began to feel how much pain Father God felt over the broken hearts of his children. As time went on, God made it clear to Denise and me that we were to leave our roles as university professors and administrators and follow his path to be agents of his healing to others.

Throughout the Scriptures, when God placed his name on something, it was always important. Prior to starting our ministry in 1995, we had no specific ministry name in mind. Then God gave me the name "The Father's Heart," and I knew it was from him. Through the years we have returned over and over to a fundamental truth: the Father is passionately pursuing each one of our hearts, and he will do whatever is necessary to recover, heal, and restore those places in our hearts that have been wounded.

During the first few years of this ministry, I (Denise) had a dream, and in it God showed me his heart. It was unbelievably big, beyond anything I could imagine. It was clear in this dream that God's heart had many expressions, and whenever God "turned his face" just a little, I could see another aspect of his heart. It was also clear that I could spend a lifetime pursuing his heart and never come to the end of the revelatory process. It seemed as though God wanted me to know two things: his heart expresses itself in a multitude of ways, and the desires of his heart for his people are endless.

From our experience working with hundreds of clients since 1995, we have seen that people's inability to love themselves has been the most significant hindrance in their ability to love God and others and to walk in freedom and wholeness.

When we love ourselves, we experience greater peace and joy in life, and we become better able to fulfill the destiny that God places within us. This powerful truth and its implications for our lives are what have inspired us to write this book.

There is another important reason for writing, and that is to clarify that this crucial need—the ability to love ourselves—is biblical. Indeed, it is more than just biblical: it is an essential truth for Christians to know, experience, and live out. Not to do so creates emotional and spiritual conflict within us. Yet many in the Christian community operate out of misunderstanding and error regarding this topic.

Although this is not a book on the theology of loving yourself, we hope to shed enough scriptural light on the subject that many who have previously rejected the notion of self-love will come to see it as essential for sound emotional and spiritual health. While this book can benefit someone who has not yet entrusted his or her heart into the care of Jesus Christ, our primary audience is those who have. In other words, we are addressing Christians—people who believe in the good news of Jesus Christ—who are unable to love themselves (and who may not even know it).

Throughout this book we will often refer to the terms *true self* and *false self* (sometimes called our *private self* and *public self*, respectively). We believe that, although many factors shape who we become as we progress from birth into adulthood, God has placed in us a core identity that he wants revealed in our lives. We also believe that this core identity is best realized when we live from our hearts, from the desires that God has placed in us, and the level of freedom that we walk in. This core, heart-based identity is what we mean when we refer to our true self.

As we progress through the formative years of childhood, we typically learn various ways of adapting to adversity. Our true self becomes covered over or even lost, and we start functioning from another identity—our false self. The false self can manifest in a multitude of ways: becoming strong and controlling, or perfectionistic and performance-driven, or passive and compliant, and so on. Many of our addictions stem from living out of our false selves. Our false self is a mask behind which we hide, often unaware that we are hiding.

But God desires something very different for us. He is calling us back to his original design for us—our true self and true heart—so we can love more freely, deeply, and effectively and fulfill our destiny that comes from within.

Since the younger, childlike parts of ourselves are usually closer to God's original intent for us, we often use those terms—*younger part* and *childlike part*—synonymously for our true self.

A book cannot replace the benefit of working one-on-one with a counselor. That said, we hope to provide a process whereby you can (1) tell whether you have a hard time loving yourself, and to what degree; (2) identify the core reasons why you don't love yourself; and (3) enter into a process whereby you can finally begin to love what God loves—YOU—and live your life from a position of security in his love.

This book is not designed to be read through like a novel; it is a road map toward wholeness and joy that may take you through difficult places, and there may be stop-off points. We encourage you to set your own pace. We realize that for some of you, this book may open up sensitive and painful issues. If you find yourself struggling with overwhelming emotions, we recommend that you stay within that section that is impacting you and slowly process the material. We also encourage you to seek additional help if you find that you need assistance working through the book. We recognize that neither the writing of this book nor the healing and wholeness we hope you'll discover through it can occur without the direct involvement of the Holy Spirit. So as we set out on this journey together, we invite you to pray with us here:

PRAYER

Lord Jesus, I invite you to direct and guide me in this time of exploration, revelation, and healing. You know everything about me, and you love me—all of me. Open my eyes to see what you would have me see and to feel what you would have me feel.

You came as the One "full of grace and full of truth." Now please give me your grace as I look further into this area of loving myself, and let me know and experience the truth of how you really see me. It is my desire to walk in greater wholeness and freedom and to ultimately love you more and bring your love to others. I trust you in this and rely on you. Amen.

Welcome to the journey. Along the way, we—Jerry and Denise—will be sharing parts of our personal stories with you as well as the stories of people with whom we have worked. We're honored that you have chosen to travel with us on this path.

CHAPTER ONE

LOVE WHAT GOD LOVES

"I just want you to kill the little girl inside me."
—Alice on her first counseling appointment

Believe it or not, that was Alice's answer to our first question on her first counseling appointment. The question was, "What do you want to see happen in your time with us so that when you leave here, you would say, 'I am glad I came?'" Imagine the look on our faces upon her response! After all, she was coming to The Father's Heart Ministry, whose very name suggests a more loving outcome than what Alice envisioned. As Alice would soon find out, the little girl inside her was the part that needed to be healed, not killed, and restored to the Father's original design.

I don't know where I (Denise) learned that it would be okay to hate myself, dislike myself, or think shaming thoughts about myself, but I am pretty sure it came with my Catholic upbringing. I was raised as a good little Catholic girl who went to confession to the priest just about every week. It went something like this, "Father, forgive me. It has been one week since my last confession. I called my sisters names four or five times. I disobeyed my parents two or three times. I lied once or twice. I am sorry for these sins and all the sins of my past life." I often made up sins and times of sins in order to make sure my confession covered all the commandments.

One traumatic day, I found a little black book in my mother's dresser drawer. It was a comprehensive (and I mean r-e-a-l-l-y comprehensive) list of all the sins you could possibly commit under each of the Ten Commandmments. I never read any further than the list under the first commandment. Ever. I was now aware of so many sins to confess to the priest that I was scared to death to read any more.

My ten-year-old sister also found the book. One night after she read it and learned how supposedly bad she was, I remember feeling terrified that she would die during the night and go to hell. I don't know what a seven-year-old knows about intercessory prayer, but I did my part praying and worrying for most of the night.

That week, not wanting to risk leaving any sinful stone unturned, my sister confessed to the priest that she had committed adultery. I guess she felt that if a sin was out there, she had probably committed it. The priest asked her, "How old are you?" He didn't say anymore when she told him she was ten. I'm pretty sure she didn't have to do any penance for that one.

At that time in my life, I tried my hardest to please God—to measure up to whatever his standard was (I was never entirely sure) and be good enough to earn his favor so bad things wouldn't happen to me or my family. I suppose I was still in the phase of childhood when I had magical thinking: when everything was focused on me and everything that happened in my world was because of me. The concept of *magical thinking*, a normal phase in a child's development, can create major problems if not recognized and addressed by astute parents.

For example, it would have been normal for me as a young child to believe that my thoughts and actions could significantly affect the lives of others—especially if I had gotten the message that God, much like Santa Claus, rewards children who are good. It naturally follows that God either punishes or withholds good things if children are *not* good. So if something goes wrong in my family—if my father is injured in a car accident or my parents can't pay the bills—then I must have done something bad or else not done something good enough, such as saying my prayers. I then try to become better or do better.

I am too young to understand the irrationality of such a belief. So if enough bad things occur for which I continue to believe I am responsible, then I will begin to believe that "I am bad," and a *core lie* will begin to take root.

Magical thinking and its consequences are separate from poor parenting behaviors such as abuse and emotional neglect. Those can make the strength of the core lies even greater. Parents can counteract some of these early, irrational beliefs if they can recognize when a child is internalizing and owning something that is not theirs to own.

Thomas is a thirty-five-year-old pastor's kid. He learned early not to shame the family. He blamed himself for the violent spankings from dad and the frequent slaps across the face from mom. He remembers sitting in his bedroom with a knife when he was five years old, trying to figure out how to kill himself. He described himself to us as being full of self-loathing. He believed God had purposely shortchanged him to keep him simple and of little value. Without the help of the Holy Spirit to search his heart, Thomas began a daily, merciless pattern of self-examination. He always found himself to be lacking and *so bad*. There wasn't a crumb of self-love anywhere.

The movie *Good Will Hunting* is worth its counseling weight in gold because of one powerful scene. (Isn't it amazing how God can use a movie with some not-so-good language to pierce our hearts and shake our beliefs about our identity?) In the scene, the psychologist, Sean (played by Robin Williams), is talking to a troubled teen, Will (played by Matt Damon), whom Sean has been counseling regarding anger issues.

Will was physically abused as a child, rejected by his father, and is heading down a bad path. The psychologist befriends him, which is not easy. Will has learned not to trust anyone; yet although his personal walls are a fortress, somehow the psychologist gets in. Here is an excerpt from the scene in the office where the two men are talking about their experiences with physical abuse:

Sean: My dad used to make us walk down to the park and collect the sticks he was going to beat us with. Actually, the worst of the beatings were between me and my brother. We would practice on each other, trying to find sticks that would break.

Will: My dad used to just put a belt, a stick, and a wrench on the kitchen table and say, "Choose." I used to go with the wrench.

Sean: I don't know a lot, Will, but let me tell you one thing—all this history (points to his file) … Look at me, son. (Both of them are looking at each other). This is not your fault.

Will: (nonchalantly) Yeah, I know.

Sean: It's not your fault.

Will: (jokingly smiling) I know.

Sean: (seriously) It's not your fault.

Will: (very agitated) Don't _____ with me, man.

Sean: (now directly in his face) It's not your fault.

Will: I know—I know.… (His heart breaks and he loses it— BUSTED).

Sean takes Will in his arms and holds him like a child. Will sobs like a baby, and after a moment, he wraps his arms around Sean and holds him even tighter. We watch a touching demonstration of two lonely people being a father and son together.

That interchange, repeated several times (kind of like Jesus asking Peter three times, "Do you love me?"), has the power and truth of God on it. Over and over again in counseling, the Holy Spirit has breathed on these words:

It's not your fault.
It's not your fault.
IT'S NOT YOUR FAULT.

In those words, God has given his children more good news, news that they previously believed was too good to be true. The Father says, "I know you, I see you, I am crazy about you, and I will heal every part of you."

You see, God wastes nothing. Nothing. Love what God loves—YOU. He doesn't hold you in contempt even though he knows everything. So why do *you* still hold yourself in contempt?

We are reminded of another movie scene, the court scene in the movie *Liar, Liar*. The lawyer (Jim Carey) is emotionally coming apart in the courtroom. The judge says, "One more outburst like that and this court will hold you in contempt." Carey follows with, "Your honor, I hold *myself* in contempt!"

Did the writer of that line eavesdrop on our counseling appointments? What a classic yet tragic conclusion so many people reach regarding themselves. This is one time when it is really good to find out you are wrong and God's opinion of you is right.

I (Denise) like to joke that my father and God are a lot alike—they both think they are always right. We will address this matter in more depth in a subsequent chapter, but since you are starting to grasp the good news of God's truth about you, why not start coming out of agreement with some of the lies you've believed right now? Using I Corinthians 13:4–8 as a template, ask yourself these questions:

- Do I love myself?
- Am I patient, gentle, and kind to myself?
- Do I easily let go of my mistakes and wrongs?
- Do I hold myself in contempt?
- Do I continually doubt or shame or berate or condemn myself?
- Do I trust myself? (A few years ago, a close friend with a prophetic gift spoke profoundly into my life. She pointed her finger at my heart and said, "Denise, the Lord is saying, 'Trust *you*.'" That statement didn't mean that I should trust in myself instead of God. Heavens no! It meant that I was to agree with how God sees me. And he sees me with a good heart that he personally placed in me).

We are now back to the original premise of this book: the missing commandment—to love my neighbor *as myself.*

What if I don't do a good job of loving myself? And what if my ability to love others can never exceed my ability to love me? How well, then, am I loving others? In reality, maybe not so well. Especially when I am just doing whatever I can to be liked, accepted, and appreciated by others; when I need their affection, attention, and approval; when I can't have anyone mad at me … in short, when I can't let anyone see the real me. The poser others see becomes a fabricated self, and once again I abandon my real self, reject myself, and shame myself. If I don't measure up enough for me, I will never be able to internalize and believe the love and care that God and others have for me.

God With Us

Hide—quick! As a little girl, Tamara used to hide in her closet, both from her parents and from God. In one of her sessions with us, we asked her if it would be okay if from now on the Father could come and sit in the closet with her. That suggestion opened up a whole new world for Tamara and shifted something in her heart. "Father God just wants to be *with* me. Is this the too-good-to-be-true good news? Wow!"

Whether God is sitting in your dark closet with you, or sitting in the corner for a time-out with you, or climbing in your make-believe tent and playing army with you; whether you are being good or getting into trouble, helping your mom bake cookies or looking at your dad's pornography magazines that you found under his bed, there is one thing that remains constant: Emmanuel, "God *with* us." The revelation of what that means, as seemingly small as Father God coming in and sitting next to you in your closet, can transform your heart forever.

When Cathy was six years old, her mother angrily pushed her out the front door and slammed it in her face. Cathy had to walk to school for school pictures. And to make matters worse, her mom had cut her bangs really short (a traumatic memory for many of us!).

In one of our sessions with Cathy, Father God showed her that he was right next to her—*with* her. She felt him take her by the hand, and he walked with her all the way to school. She thought he would just drop her off there, but instead he stayed with her, and in doing so revealed his protection of her.

This revelation of God's constant care and companionship transformed Cathy's painful memory of her mother's actions. It was no longer buried or stuffed inside of her, still alive with rejection, hurt, and shame. Instead, it was dead, buried, and replaced with a warm knowledge of the Father's presence. And from this place of God's loving presence, Cathy was able to forgive her mother and take her off the hook. This memory is now part of Cathy's story of how God met her with his love and grace. It is another example of the Father restoring the years of our past that "the locusts have eaten" (Joel 2:25).

This one word, *with*, has impacted my (Denise's) understanding of God and is changing the way I envision him and present him to others during counseling. Emmanuel, "God with us," is not with us merely in a general, God-is-everywhere way, but in a specific and intentional next-to-us way. He is a Father who is touching us shoulder to shoulder. He comes alongside us and puts his arm around us. He is playing in the sand with us, hiding in the closet with us so we don't have to be scared and alone. He is walking hand in hand with us, protecting us and standing up for us, weeping with us when someone close to us hurts us or even violates us, grieving with us when we hurt ourselves with our own self-hatred.

In all these things and more, our Father's love remains constant. It never changes—not with one good work or a thousand, not with one sin or a million. After the prodigal son in Luke chapter 15 committed every wrong in the book, the father wouldn't even hear his "I'm sorry." The father watched for his son to return, and when he finally saw him, he picked up his long robe and ran as fast as he could to him. He embraced his wayward son, kissed his stinkiness, welcomed him, brought gifts for him, celebrated him, poured out his heart over him, wept for joy because of him, forgave him, set a place of honor for him, and called all his friends to share the good news of his son's homecoming. This is the same Father who never stops believing in us and never stops making plans for us: plans to heal, restore, and free us and guide us into the identity and destiny he wove into us in our mother's womb.

The story of the prodigal son confronts us with God's kindness—the kindness that leads us to repentance. One of the hugest things I lose out on when I fail to love myself is a revelation of that kindness and of the gift of repentance (Romans 2:4). How very sad for me! I am too busy accusing myself and trying to make myself better next time so I can be pleasing to God and earn his blessing. Try on this scenario and see if it fits:

I sin.

I'm sorry.

I sin again.

I won't do it anymore.

I sin again.

I'll try harder. (Is that working for you?)

Now comes the negative self-talk.

I am so frustrated with myself. I'm a loser, a screw-up.

Next, I get mad at God.

Why aren't you helping me?

Finally, I draw my conclusion.

I can't, God won't, so why try? I guess God is there for everyone else, but not for me.

Our client Liz told us about a conversation she had with her sister. Liz said to her sister, "I know that God loves you and is there for you, but he doesn't care about me." Her sister responded, "How can you say that? It is so obvious to me that he totally loves you and has been helping you. I just can't believe he loves me."

It was one of those God-breaks-in moments for Liz. "Hmm," Liz pondered. "So we both are absolutely sure that God loves the other one and is there for her. If we both really believe this in our hearts, and if we both are right, then both of us have to be wrong about God not loving each of us personally. Since I am so sure that God loves and cares for *you*, I have to believe he also loves and cares for *me*."

Beth Moore, in her book *Breaking Free*, tells the story of a group of women she was teaching about God's love. She asked them to each look into the eyes of the person next to them and say, "God loves *me* so much." Guess what happened all over the room? Moore writes, "The women turned to one another and said, 'God loves *you* so much.'"[1]

What a perfect example of how we accept God's love for others but struggle to believe in his love for us. Yet the truth is, *God loves me just as much as he loves others—equally, radically, completely, and unfailingly.*

Why do we believe otherwise? Why do we change the very words and heart of the Father? Say this sentence out loud: "I have loved you _____ (your name) with an everlasting love." You have just personalized the very words of God written in Jeremiah 31:3. Wow! What if we could say that about ourselves every day? Unfortunately, we can always make a case against ourselves because we know our own sins and weaknesses and struggles all too well.

Jerry and I ache in our hearts during our counseling sessions when we hear the personal stories of those sitting on the couch across the room from us. How honored we are that couples and individuals have found a safe place with us to share their deep pain. We can see and feel the trauma of their struggles. But even more than that—I, Denise, can feel the tears welling up as I write—we feel the pain of Father God longing for our counselees to know his love and the truth about how he sees them.

The "Missing" Commandment

In Mark 12:28–31, Jesus is asked which of the commandments is the most important. He replies, "Love the Lord your God with all your heart and with all your soul and with all your mind and with all your strength." He continues, "The second is this: 'Love your neighbor as yourself.' There is no commandment greater than these."

In his first command about loving God, Jesus references Deuteronomy 6:5. In his second command about loving others as ourselves, he quotes from Leviticus 19:18. The importance of these two statements stands out even more clearly in Matthew 22:40 when Jesus declares, "All the Law and the Prophets hang on these two commandments." There is nothing more important in either the Old or the New Testaments of the Bible, in terms of what God asks of us, than to love him and to love others *as we love ourselves.*

We seem to get most of this. We are to love God and we are to love others. But where Jerry and I see so many falling short on understanding and living out this teaching is in the area of "loving yourself."

Ask yourself, "Do I love others to the same degree or in the way or manner that I love myself?" The equation looks like this:

My love for others is neither less nor greater than my love for myself.
My love for others is equal to my love for myself.

There is no difference. None. **We believe that loving yourself is the missing commandment.**

We are not saying it is missing from the Bible or from the teachings of Christ. It is clearly present. Rather, we believe it is missing in great part in the church and in the lives of those who seek to follow Christ. We further believe—based on our own lives and the lives of those we have counseled—that it is not possible to do a good job of keeping the first commandment, loving God, without fulfilling all of the second.

Healing the Brokenhearted and Loving What God Loves

Recently, at a teaching facility in the Midwest, the presence of God fell on a classroom of college students. Twelve hours later, no one had left the room because of what God was doing. Report after report came from individuals who were being touched by God in a profound way. He was healing them of self-hatred. Of guilt. Of shame.

Physical healings do not always change the heart of a person, but what unfathomable freedom can come when God heals a broken heart.

We see an example of this in Luke 17:11–19 when Jesus healed the ten men with leprosy but only one "came back, praising God in a loud voice" and thanking Jesus. In contrast, when Jesus spoke with the woman at the well in John 4:1–42, his prophetic words about the condition of her life and heart resulted in a heart change. She *had* to tell others what had happened to her. John 4:39 states that "many of the Samaritans from that town believed in him because of the woman's testimony, 'He told me everything I ever did.'" Maybe, if you too could experience the heart change offered by Jesus, you could respond by loving what he loves—YOU.

We started our ministry with the first and greatest commandment as the center of everything we set out to accomplish. We wanted to help others love God with their whole heart and remove from their hearts anything—pain, hurt, betrayal, fear, wounds, walls—that hindered the free expression of that love. Somewhere in the midst of our ministry's formative period, Father God turned the page to the second commandment. Let us explain using the story of a young woman we counseled back then.

Janet had dedicated her life to the Lord in her late teens and dreamed of evangelizing the world for Jesus. She was an intercessor and worshipper and really, really loved God. Yet when we asked her to describe how God saw her, she said that she chose not to think of his love for her. As a worship leader, Janet skipped the songs that spoke of her being God's favorite, his beloved, or of her being beautiful and precious to him.

Janet wasn't alone. We began to hear this kind of story again and again—statements like …

"I really love God, but I don't feel he loves me."
"I'm disappointed with myself, and I feel that God, too, is disappointed with me."
"I know that God loves others, but I don't sense his love for me."
"I feel that God is distant and disinterested in me."

"I know in my head that God loves me, but I don't feel it in my heart."

"I don't feel God's love, and actually, I don't feel much of anything."

These statements are only a few of many similar ones that have come our way. We know that the Father grieves over them and desires to help his children love what he himself loves so deeply—themselves.

How Good Is the Good News?

I (Denise) remember only one sermon from when I was growing up. I was seven years old, and I was sitting in the pew doing the usual things to stay quiet and out of trouble, like polishing my patent leather shoes with a hankie. A young Catholic priest from the Jesus movement was giving the message at our church. I remember him saying emphatically, "Jesus loves you."

Huh? What was that? My shoe polishing ceased while I took it in. Jesus *loves* me? With all the rules and shoulds and oughts I was working on in order to be good, stay out of trouble, and avoid punishment, that thought had never crossed my mind.

Today, our entire lives and ministry are wrapped up in that one sentence: Jesus loves you. It is profoundly good news. The following story demonstrates the life-changing impact of that good news for one of our clients when he experienced heart-to-heart connection with the Father. One word sums it up best: Wow!

All Raymond ever wanted was to be cared for and to have a sense of belonging. His dad "wasn't around" until Raymond was twelve years old. As for his mom, Raymond felt that he was just in her way. She would send him out the kitchen door in the morning with a stern, "Now get outside," and she wouldn't let him back in the house until dinnertime.

As we began praying with Raymond against the lies he believed about himself . . .

I don't belong
My feelings don't count
If you really knew me, you wouldn't like me
I can never measure up

. . . Raymond started to hear the Father's voice. God's words came against all of the lies that were embedded deeply in his heart for as long as he could remember. With tears and excitement, Raymond began telling us what God was saying:

"Oh my gosh! God cares what I feel!"

"It's not my fault!" (*"This is mind blowing!"*)

"I have a good heart!"

"He likes what he made! Wow!"

"I don't have to do anything! I'm valued just for being me!"

"I am his son!"

"He just wants to be with me! Wow!"

Suddenly, Raymond had a memory of playing outside with his Hot Wheels cars. In the past, this had been one of the things he did all alone when his mother sent him outside for hours. This time, though, the Father went out the screen door with him, sat down, and started drawing roads in the sand for his cars.

At this point, Raymond's childlike awe and exuberance were filling up the atmosphere in the counseling room. His excitement was contagious. He started sharing more revelations from God, and after each one he kept saying, "Wow!"

What makes Raymond's experience even more special is that he had never before felt God's love tangibly. At the beginning of our time together, he told us, "I must be one of those people who just doesn't get it. I ask for a personal experience with God, but I walk away disappointed."

The next day, Raymond and his wife left us the best card we had ever received. It said, simply, "Thank you so much . . . and WOW!"

Another story of a longstanding client provides a beautiful demonstration of how God heals us as we learn to love ourselves. Patrice had a severe eating disorder. One day, as she was going into the bathroom at work to purge her lunch, she heard God say in her spirit, "I want you to look in the mirror and say, 'I love you, Patrice.'"

She said it was one of the hardest things she ever had to do. She did it anyway, because she believed it was God telling her to do it. And a powerful thing happened: the urge to purge vanished.

"I love you, Patrice," continues to be a powerful prayer in her life—and in the lives of other clients. I, Denise, have walked many over to a large mirror outside my office, had them look themselves straight in the eyes, and then encouraged them to verbalize a love for themselves that agrees with God's own deep love for them. This prayer of declaring our love for ourselves is one of the hardest and most powerful prayers we can pray to break lies and strongholds and to free our hearts to love.

God desires to heal our self-hatred, self-condemnation, self-contempt, self-deprecation, and negative self-talk. When we come into agreement with who the Father says we are as his beloved children—and when we are able to love ourselves the way he loves us—we also become better able to trust his heart and to love others in return.

As Jerry and I have walked through our own journeys of healing, we have had to ask ourselves many different questions:

- When did I learn to strive, to perform, to look and act a certain way in order to earn approval or avoid conflict?
- When did I start saying yes when I needed to say no?
- When did I begin hiding the real me because I felt inadequate, insecure, guilty, alone, unloved, self-contemptuous, and unable to measure up?
- When did I decide in my heart that I would never be weak, that I would always be in control, that I would never let anyone know I was hurting?

Finding answers to questions like these is a doorway into the journey of healing.

An Exclamation Point from God

A few months ago, we went to see our financial advisor to discuss our retirement plans. We had never met him before, and he knew little about us and our counseling ministry. At our second meeting, we shared with him our focus on healing past hurts, just general heart-healing small talk.

Our advisor leaned into the table toward us and told the following story. It felt like a hold-your-breath God-moment, and we both listened intently.

Fifteen years ago, he took his daughter to hear a guest speaker at his church's youth ministry. The speaker was in his late twenties, dressed in faded jeans and flip-flops, and he strummed his guitar while he spoke. He said he had noticed how Christians are encouraged and expected to love others—to serve and help and volunteer. But what about the Scripture that says we are supposed to love others *as we love ourselves*? Why were Christians failing to love themselves, and why was no one even talking about that "missing piece"?

Our financial advisor said that the young man's statement really impacted him, and it still does today, fifteen years later.

It was one of those *aha!* moments, a God-fingerprint that marked his heart. We could hardly contain ourselves as we, in turn, shared about the book we planned to write and the title God had given me (Denise): *The Missing Commandment—Love Yourself.* It was great to experience such a God-right-with-us moment.

The Heart of the Father for You

Here is a journal entry which Father God spoke to my spirit as I (Denise) prepared to write this book:

You are my voice spoken into the wilderness in my children's hearts. Tell them again how I feel about them, that I am crazy about them. Tell them I am LOVE. Tell them there is more good news and that they can live, really live LIFE, from this news. May their hearts expand beyond imagination when you tell them what they thought was too good to be true about themselves. When they believe loving themselves is arrogant and prideful and selfish, it wars against my very heart. Tell them. Tell them. I will open a realm in my children to see and feel my heart. They will never be the same. This is my gift to them that releases their true identity and destiny. No one can stop my heart.

Loving what God loves is the key—and yes, he absolutely loves you.

PRAYER

Father, open my heart and help me see what you want me to see concerning this issue of loving myself. As I begin this journey into my heart, I need to know more of your heart. Help me to see if this commandment has been missing in my life, and if so, help me to find and restore that which has been lost or disregarded. You pursue lost things (Luke 15), and you pursue me so that I can live from a restored heart. I want to be able to fully love you, myself, and others. I trust you in this journey. In Jesus's name, amen.

QUESTIONS FOR REFLECTION

1. What would you hope to discover in reading this book on loving yourself so that when you finish the last page you could say, "I'm really glad I read this"?

2. Do you find that you are the one who is hardest on yourself? Share examples from your life story.

3. What do you believe about this statement: "God doesn't hold me in contempt even though he knows everything about me"? Assuming the statement is true, how do you get around it when you are harboring contempt for yourself?

4. How did you respond to the questions we asked earlier in reference to 1 Corinthians 13?
   • Do I love myself?
   • Am I patient, gentle, and kind to myself?
   • Do I easily let go of my mistakes and wrongs?
   • Do I hold myself in contempt?
   • Do I continually doubt or shame or berate or condemn myself?
   • Do I trust myself?

5. Ponder this question in your heart: What would change for you if your perception of Emmanuel, "God with us," shifted from a general, God-is-everywhere perspective to a personal view of "God with *me*"? Right next to me. Arm around me. Always. Never moving. Never changing. Never giving up on me. Loving me. *Always.* If your heart could see God in this manner, how might things be different for you?

6. Reflect on your responses to these questions:
   • When did I learn to strive, to perform, to look and act a certain way in order to earn approval or avoid conflict?
   • When did I start saying yes when I needed to say no?
   • When did I begin hiding the real me because I felt inadequate, insecure, guilty, alone, unloved, self-contemptuous, and unable to measure up?

- When did I decide in my heart that I would never be weak, that I would always be in control, that I would never let anyone know I was hurting?

7. Reread the prayer that preceded these questions, or write your own. You may want to keep a journal close at hand as you proceed on this healing journey.

CHAPTER TWO

"BUT WOULDN'T THAT BE SELFISH?"

*—The response from a friend when we told him
we were writing a book on loving yourself*

Scripture is very clear regarding the command to love and serve others. The apostle Paul wrote in Romans 12:10, "Be devoted to one another in brotherly love. Honor one another above yourselves." Again, in 1 Corinthians 13:5—the well-known "love chapter"—he wrote, "[Love] is not self-seeking."

Our ultimate model of selfless love is Christ as he laid down his life for us so that we might have life (Ephesians 5:2). Jesus also spoke clearly on what is required in order for a person to be one of his disciples: "He [or she] must deny himself and take up his cross daily and follow me. For whoever wants to save his life will lose it, but whoever loses his life for me will save it" (Luke 9:23–24).

So doesn't it seem backwards or selfish to focus on loving ourselves instead of loving and serving others? Many people, especially non-Christians, would argue that the commandment that is in fact "missing" from the Christian life is the loving of others. Unfortunately, there is more truth in this statement than most of us care to admit.

But if that is so, then what is the answer? Do I simply decide to love and serve more? Do I need to hear another sermon on loving, serving, and giving, and then I will finally understand and be able to step out and do those things more? Or do I need to refresh myself on what the Scriptures say about dying to self and loving my neighbor and then just start applying what I read?

Emphatically, NO.

We in no way want to minimize the importance of translating our faith into action (James 2:17). Moreover, we do not believe there is only one explanation for why so many Christians fall short in that area. We do believe, however, that our ability to love ourselves has a great impact on how well we love others. If learning to love myself better ultimately enables me to love *you* better, then the result is definitely not selfish.

In *Waking the Dead*, John Eldredge says it this way:

> Caring for our own hearts isn't selfishness; it's how we begin to love. Yes, we care for our hearts for the sake of others. Does that sound like a contradiction? Not at all. What will you bring to others if your heart is empty, dried up, pinned down? Love is the point. And you can't love without your heart, and you can't love well unless your heart is well....
>
> How you handle your own heart is how you will handle [other people's]. If you dismiss your heart, you will end up dismissing theirs. If you expect perfection of your heart, you will raise that same standard for them. If you manage your heart for efficiency and performance, that is what you'll pressure them to be.[2]

Even though we are often harder on ourselves then we are on others, lack of love for ourselves will eventually manifest in how we relate to others.

In the words of Jesus, "If your first concern is to look after yourself, you'll never find yourself. But if you forget about yourself and look to me, you'll find both yourself and me" (Matthew 10:39 MSG). Perhaps you, like many Christians, understand that verse as saying that you should ignore your struggles and needs and do whatever it takes to "get past self and press in to God." To us, though, this scriptural paradox has a different meaning which makes all the sense in the world. If you try through your own efforts to get yourself right enough, clean enough, spiritual enough, pleasing enough to go to God, you'll never get there. But if you come in the simplicity, vulnerability, and honesty of a child (your true self), you will find him. And when you find him, you will also find yourself—because you are already *in* him, hidden in Christ and in the Father's heart. In Luke 14:11 MSG, Jesus promises that "if you're content to be simply yourself, you will become more than yourself."

How Pure Is Your Love?

Both as counselors and as long-time members of the Christian community, we have often observed two responses to giving and serving. One is from church members who have been "doing" for a long time. They often become tired, weary, burned out, and even resentful from devoting so much of themselves to their church's volunteer ministries. They cannot or do not want to keep up the pace, but they feel guilty when they stop.

The other response is from people who have chosen to give or serve very little and feel unmotivated to do so. They often become disillusioned and discouraged in their walk of faith.

Each kind of person truly loves God, yet neither experiences his love in return.

In getting to the root of these conditions, we often encounter *love deficits:* places within a person that did not receive enough love in the individual's early, formative years. Love deficits may arise from a lack of loving actions shown to a child, or they may be the result of negative or abusive acts or words directed at the child. In any case, as such individuals come into adulthood, they begin to perform and give from the place of their unmet needs for love. On the surface, their actions seem good and loving; such people appear caring, sacrificial, accepting, and giving. However, what may actually be driving their actions is a need for love and affection, a fear of rejection, a desire for acceptance, a hunger for attention, or a desperate need for belonging and security.

Alfred Ells describes this style of relating as follows:

We learn to please and care for others in order to win love or avoid pain. We don't want others to reject or hurt us, so we go to extra lengths to love them. We don't want to feel the pain of our children's failures, so we go to great lengths to make them succeed. We love too much because we need too much to be loved. And we care too much because we need care.[3]

Joe was a young man who grew up with a raging father. Joe experienced a lot of yelling and a lot of cursing. He learned to read the atmosphere in the room and keep the peace whenever possible. Following his father's outbursts, Joe was always there to comfort his mother. He felt close to his mom, and in the process of caring for her, he unknowingly made himself responsible for her happiness.

In return, his mom showed him great love and care. But deep inside his heart, Joe was developing a love deficit. Although his mom didn't realize it, her actions and attitudes toward her son were tainted by her own need for his love and care, and the flow of love often went in the wrong direction—toward Mom. Joe's mother never realized that her own damaged ability to love, care, and give was coming from an unresolved, hurtful past that still controlled her relationships.

The bottom line from Joe's story is that, unless they are detected, unmet needs create unhealthy styles of relating, first between parent and child and then extending to relationships with self, God, and others. Because Joe's father and mother, and ultimately Joe himself were unable to love themselves, the love they gave to others was not pure.

But the good news is, although much damage can result from growing up with love deficits, Joe and many like him have found healing and restoration. The broken places within us respond to the healing love of our heavenly Father—a Father who cares deeply about our past and its impact on us today.

A Martyr

I don't know exactly when, but sometime during my childhood, I (Denise) began taking on the problems and burdens of others. I always befriended the underdog and the outcast. I read every book on the lives of the saints in our Catholic school library, and I was ready to lay down my life in order to deny myself and prefer others. There was just one huge missing piece: I didn't have a self to lay down.

Let me say that in another way: a child who gets lost in order to please others does not have anything to truly give away. I needed to find my true self—the identity God knit within me—before I could love others in fullness. Jesus never wavered in who he was, and thus he had a self he could deny and sacrifice for others. I, on the other hand, had made a martyr of myself before I had a self to be martyred. And I did it in my own strength of being "good" (the enemy of being God's *best*).

A Nice Guy

It took many years for me to realize that I (Jerry) operated out of my unmet needs, which shaped many of my actions. I was what many would consider a "nice guy." But in reality, my heart wasn't so nice. Because of some core love deficits that only became known to me in my middle thirties, much of my love for others was driven by my own needs for acceptance. I became a people-pleaser and a peacekeeper, and I did whatever was necessary to avoid relational conflicts. I operated out of what is called a *shame-based identity*, which was built on a core of lies, mainly concerning myself.

As we will explain in greater detail in a later chapter, unhealthy shame, which is established very early in childhood, says that there is something inherently wrong, flawed, or defective in me, and if you really knew me, you would not like me. As a result of believing this, I either grow up seeking to prove that I am okay (and not allowing anyone to see that I am not), or else I grow up with a defeatist attitude and give up on trying to prove that I'm okay. I chose the former, performance-based route. Although I enjoyed success, I operated unknowingly from an unhealthy place, and my driving needs remained unmet.

At my core, I did not know I was okay—in fact, I believed quite the opposite—and, as a result, I did not love myself and was unable to genuinely love others. I often would do loving things, but my actions had the wrong motivation.

You can imagine how this dysfunction manifested in my marriage with Denise. For many years, she wanted more of my heart, but I was unable to offer it to her. I couldn't be emotionally intimate with her because I didn't even know my own heart. It was occupied by too much false self, and intimacy requires truth in the innermost parts. Only after entrusting my heart to Christ and allowing him to find the real Jerry could the healing work begin.

I feel grateful that I am no longer the "nice guy" (aka "the poser") I used to be. Today I operate much more from my true, God-created self. Dealing with my shame and its underlying lies was huge. As I began to let God pour his love into places within me that desperately needed it, I also had to learn to love myself—especially my younger self—for the healing to be most effective.

Disagreeing with the Father

Ironically, when we do not love ourselves, we actually become more selfish. As Denise and I have shared in our stories, our actions became a means to get our own needs met—needs for acceptance, security, love—instead of loving others.

Consciously or often unconsciously, we interact with people not because we love so deeply, but because we need something in return. Yet at the same time, we build walls of protection that keep others outside of our heart. Thus we become even more selfish. Also, there is another relationship that is negatively affected when we operate from past hurts and fail to love ourselves: our relationship with God.

When we adopt various methods of coping with unhealed places within us, we severely hinder our ability to feel and experience the heart of Father God. Since he created us for intimate relationship with himself, he will pursue us and do whatever is necessary to restore that intimacy. By not loving ourselves, we disagree with how he sees us and feels about us. We end up actually opposing him—unintentionally, of course; nevertheless, when our self-assessment becomes more important to us than the Father's assessment of us, then our actions become self-centered rather than God-centered.

Thank God there is a road out of this unhealthy place! The first step is to recognize that loving yourself as the Father loves you is not a selfish act. To do otherwise is to disagree with the Father—and the Father is always right.

P R A Y E R

Father, show me how you see me and how you feel about me. Help me to see if my view of myself is different from yours— if there are parts of me, parts of my very heart, that I do not love. I want to be in agreement with you. I want to love what you love. If I have felt that it was in any way wrong and selfish to look at myself in this way or to love myself, I recognize that these thoughts are not from you.

Father, I trust you in this process and believe that you will guide me as I open myself to you and allow you full access to my heart. In Jesus's name, amen.

QUESTIONS FOR REFLECTION

1. Reflect on the following statements. Share what you personally believe about the concept of loving yourself.
   - If I love myself better, I will be able to love others better.
   - If I love myself less, I will have a greater capacity to love others.
   - Caring for our own hearts isn't selfish; it's how we begin to love.
   - If I expect myself to perform and be perfect, I will undoubtedly expect others to do the same.

2. Can you tell when someone gives to you simply because they enjoy blessing you versus when someone gives with a need or expectation attached? How do each of the two motives make you feel?

3. As a Christ-follower, ponder the difference between being in a community of "nice" people versus a community of "real" people. At this time in your life, which one do you prefer? And why?

4. How is your relationship with God affected if you have not learned to love yourself?

5. Reread the prayer that preceded these questions or write your own. Make notes of any questions you may need to ask yourself or God about loving yourself.

CHAPTER THREE

COME AS A CHILD

Consider the incredible love that the Father has shown us in allowing us to be called "children of God"—and that is not just what we are called, but who we are.
—1 John 3:1 J.B. Phillips

Of all the Scriptures the Father has emphasized in our healing ministry, some of the most profound have related to coming to him as a child. No matter how old we get, the Father still refers to us as children. He adopts us as his own, and even if we surrender our lives to God at seventy years of age, we are to come as a child. After all, in our culture we adopt children, not adults, and that's how it is with God.

Jesus was very clear on his position regarding children and the kingdom of God. Mark 10:13–16 in *The Message* states,

> The people brought children to Jesus, hoping he might touch them. The disciples shooed them off. But Jesus was irate and let them know it: "Don't push these children away. Don't ever get between them and me. These children are at the very center of life in the kingdom. Mark this: Unless you accept God's kingdom in the *simplicity of a child*, you'll never get in." Then, gathering the children up in his arms, he laid his hands of blessing on them. (Emphasis added.)

Let's read this again. Stop and imagine the tone, the volume, the eyes, and the facial and body expressions of Jesus as he addresses the disciples.

Once you've done this, move to the position of seeing Jesus tenderly turning to the children. Watch him hold each one, touch each one, bless each one. Stop and feel the love that comes from his heart.

Now allow yourself to be one of those little ones that he is gathering to himself. Notice that they've done nothing to earn his love. *They just are their true selves.*

During the ministry of Jesus, he only did what his Father was doing (John 5:19). When we see Jesus, we see the Father (John 14:9). So when Jesus expresses the importance of children and childlikeness, it is because they are dear to the heart of the Father.

Putting Away Childish Things

Paul the apostle wrote, "When I was a child, I spoke as a child, I understood as a child, I thought as a child; but when I became a man, I put away childish things" (1 Corinthians 13:11 NKJV). Using this Scripture as a guide, let's look at some examples of the types of childish things we are to put away.

When I was a child, I …
- *spoke as a child*—"That's mine." "You can't have any." "I'm going to tell." "Mom, he's touching me." "Stay on your own side."
- *understood as a child*—"He touched me first." "It's his fault." "He started it." "Why can't I go?" "Why does she get to go?" "That's not fair."
- *thought as a child*—"If mom and dad are unhappy, it must be my fault." "If I try harder to be really good, they won't be mad anymore." "If I were a boy/girl, they would love me."

In adulthood, childishness shows up when you have to have your own way or the last word; when you are stubborn, unreasonable, or mean; when you bully others, throw tantrums, or display outbursts of emotion. Or perhaps you are timid and fearful and insecure—afraid to make friends (they may not like you) or afraid to raise your hand or give a different opinion (you might ask a stupid question or give the wrong answer). Then again, maybe you became a little adult early on and were very responsible for your age. You learned how to look good in front of others. All of the above are childish things to put away.

The Beauty of a Childlike Heart

While there's no virtue in being child*ish*, there are child*like* characteristics that we should never outgrow. They are always to be our true nature before the Father. As his child, God wants us to be *vulnerable*, in a position of needing his care and protection. Although we may learn that vulnerability sets us up to be hurt, the Father asks that we present ourselves with all our walls and defenses down—*trusting* that he is with us, that he knows us, loves us, and enjoys us.

A child is *imperfect* and remains imperfect throughout life. Perfection is who God is and is not anything for us to strive to become.

A child is *spontaneous* and *creative*—made in the very likeness of our Creator Father.

A child is *not fully developed*. Children need to be given the message that it is okay to learn and grow as a natural part of their lives. As children of God, we are always in a process of growth, which our Father accepts and understands.

A child is *dependent*, with needs and wants that should be recognized and acknowledged—needs such as love, affection, acceptance, and a sense of belonging. God highly esteems dependence as a characteristic of our ongoing condition and position with him. We never outgrow our need to lean on him, to be weak so that he can be strong on our behalf.

A child is *valuable, unique* and *special* to God Himself. He planned for us from the beginning and knit us together in our mother's womb. There has never been and will never be another one like us.

Some refer to this childlike part in us as our *true self,* our *private self,* the *child within,* or the *inner child.* Whatever we call it, we all can acknowledge that there is more going on in us than we realize. Henri Nouwen, in his book *The Inner Voice of Love,* refers to the inner child as our lamb.

> There is within you a lamb and a lion. Spiritual maturity is the ability to let lamb and lion lie down together. Your lion is your adult, aggressive self. It is your initiative-taking and decision-making self. But there is also your fearful, vulnerable lamb, the part of you that needs affection, support, affirmation and nurturing. Developing your identity as a *child* of God in no way means giving up your responsibilities. Likewise, claiming your adult self in no way means that you cannot become increasingly a *child* of God. In fact, the opposite is true. The more you can feel safe as a *child* of God, the freer you will be to claim your mission in the world as a responsible human being. And the more you claim that you have a unique task to fulfill for God, the more open you will be to letting your deepest need be met.[4] (Emphases added.)

Our Spirit (and Heart) within Us

We can also refer to the child part within us as our spirit, as we consist of body, soul, and spirit (Hebrews 4:12). It is our spirit—which is breathed into us by God at conception and leaves our body upon our death—that is aware of everything that has ever happened over the course of our lives.

Scripture often uses the word *heart* when referring to our spirit. Mike Mason, in his excellent book *The Mystery of Children,* states the following regarding this issue of spirit/heart:

Jesus wants us to become like children because our spirits lived closest to the surface during our childhood. In childhood our hearts are the most transparent, most vulnerable, most malleable. Growing up usually means covering up our spirit more and more with flesh. God wants us to become the person we really are inside, the person we were born to be. Becoming childlike involves peeling away the masks to get back to the real, rosy-cheeked, bright-eyed face beneath.[5]

John Eldredge, in his book *The Way of the Wild Heart*, shares about this concept, using the primary character in the movie *Antwone Fisher* to make his point.

In his nightly dreams, Antwone sees himself as a young boy, five or six years old. That was the time in his life when his heart was broken. That is how old he feels when he allows himself to feel the anguish buried inside. I believe it is more than a feeling. I believe there is part of his soul [or spirit/heart] that is six or seven. When devastating things happen to us—especially when we are young—they have the power to break our hearts. Literally. Something in the soul is shattered, and it remains stuck at the age it was when the blow came....

Haven't you had that experience, when suddenly some part of you feels very young? Maybe somebody gets mad at you, threatens to leave you—just like what happened when you were a boy. Maybe you've been asked to give a talk before a crowd, and something in you freezes. A group of men are laughing and joking easily, but you just can't join in. Something happens that was all too much like something that hurt you when you were young and in that moment, you don't feel much like a man at all. You feel like a boy inside. The reason you feel this way is that some part of you is still a boy.[6]

Our Picture of God

God makes us totally dependent on parents or caregivers for the first five years of our lives. Our parents become like gods to us. In a perfect world, this would be a good thing.

Now, let us paint a scene that happens when a child reaches five years of age. The child goes up to his mom and dad and asks, "Mommy and Daddy, what is God like?" (Even if this question never gets voiced aloud, the child's spirit will ask it and draw its own conclusions). The parents might look at their child and say, "You know, God is a lot like us—he is loving and kind and patient. He is proud of you and is always there when you need him. You are a treasure to him and he loves you no matter what. He likes to spend time with you and he sings a special song over you at night that is just for you. And out of his love, he disciplines you to help you grow."

Imagine the wide-eyed child who hears these words from his mom and dad. Wow! This is great news, almost too good to be true. With parents like these, can you see how easy the transition would be to how that child sees Father God?

It is a daunting responsibility to know that as parents and caregivers, we mirror God to a child. This means we will need to depend on God a lot (and that is what he wants).

In counseling, we see people from all walks of life who have a distorted view of God the Father because their parents misrepresented him. It doesn't matter whether the client is a missionary, pastor, music leader, or doctor of theology. *The biggest influence on how a person sees God is not their knowledge of the Scriptures. It is the representation or misrepresentation of God, which that person saw mirrored by their parents.*

We can't begin to count the number of people who have told us, "I know in my head that God loves me, but I don't feel it in my heart." This is the great disconnect that the Father wants to deal with in each one of us.

One pastor, after counseling with us for a week, vulnerably shared in his Sunday message that even though he knew God loved him, for the first time he experienced a profound revelation of "Jesus loves me, this I know" deep within his heart. Wow! To say he was transformed by his experience doesn't do it justice. This is the Father's really, *r-e-a-l-l-y* good news in action.

Another counselee, a Christian leader in business, had a personal experience in which God showed her how he celebrated her when she was born, even though no one else did. This woman shared with us that prior to her conception, her mother had lost two babies at or just after birth, and the doctor had informed her parents not to expect that this third child would live. As a result, they did not do the typical planning for her infancy. She wasn't given a name, and no crib, diapers, or newborn sleepers were purchased for her. Her parents didn't acknowledge her in the hospital nursery for three days after she was born because they believed she was going to die. This early wound of abandonment impacted her profoundly.

But God came to our client in a deep and personal way and brought healing to her spirit. When she shared with her husband the unbelievable joy and love God had shown her in her heart, she said to him, "This counseling is either kindergarten (back to "Jesus loves me, this I know") or a PhD in his love." In God's school of the Spirit, we're sure it's both.[7]

When Ted remembers the critical words his dad said to him, he hears it with the sound of a horse rawhide whip—*snap!* "Get over it." *Snap!* "Rub some dirt in it and go on." *Snap!* "That didn't hurt." *Snap!* "Quit crying, you baby." *Snap!* "I'll give you something to cry about." *Snap!* "Suck it up like a man." *Snap!* "You are an embarrassment to the family." *Snap!* "You are just a mamma's boy." *Snap!*

As he grew up, Ted picked up the rawhide lessons from dad and used the whip on himself. *Snap!*

Now his heart doesn't need a Band-Aid. It needs surgery to remove the damaged tissue and restore blood flow to the part that hardened long ago. In order to look good enough on the outside, Ted learned to perform. Not only did he demand perfection from himself, but he expected it from others as well. Now at forty-nine years of age, his internal world is falling apart. All of a sudden, Ted feels fatigued, depressed, and overwhelmed. For the first time, he can't keep all his plates spinning and hold all his beach balls under the water.

Is it any wonder that Ted has problems believing God is really there with him and for him—that God delights in him, brags about him, enjoys every little detail about him; that God knows every single hair on Ted's head; that he was intimately involved in every detail of creating Ted unique, knitting him together for nine months in his mother's womb?

Ted is at the beginning—the first steps in recovery. He is now ready to admit that his life is out of control and he is powerless over his dysfunctional behaviors and irrational beliefs. If he could overcome his problems by himself as he did in the past, he would—but he can't. Ted now turns to the Father with a heart yielded and emptied of pride, seeing his false public self, his self-deception, his weakness, and his inadequacy. Once again he finds himself coming as if he were three years old—hungry, thirsty, poor, and needy. As he lays down his independence, he finds himself right in the Father's lap, a place of dependence he never needs to leave again.

Assessing Your View of Father God

Here is an exercise that is often helpful in connecting the dots as to how parents during our developmental years can impact our view of God as adults. Carefully consider the following lists of descriptions as you complete the sentences below:

- Growing up, I saw my father as _____.
- Growing up, I saw my mother as _____.
- Today, I see Father God as _____.

Distant and indifferent	or	Close and interested
Insensitive and inconsiderate	or	Caring and compassionate
Harsh, demanding, and unreasonable	or	Considerate, kind, and gentle
Aloof and detached	or	Interested and involved

Intolerant and impatient	or	Supportive and patient
Angry, mean, and punishing	or	Loving, understanding, and protective
Controlling and manipulative	or	Gracious and merciful
Condemning or accusing	or	Forgiving and tender
Critical or perfectionistic	or	Encouraging and affirming

The harder it is for you to feel in your heart (not just know in your mind) that God is like the descriptions in the column on the right, the more you need healing for your childhood wounds. Many people have come to us over the years because they want to have a deeper relationship with God. If that is you, our prescription for helping you is not found in more Bible reading, more devotions, or more verse memorization. It is found in allowing the Father to reveal the roots of hurt, fear, rejection, and shame and letting him heal your heart—the heart of a child—so you can ultimately "come as a child" to him.

Letter to a Lost Boy

One way we suggest for our counselees to help themselves come to God as a child is for them to affirm the child within by writing to him or her. Here is a letter that one of our counselees wrote after realizing his lack of love or care for himself and its impact on his life as an adult:

Little Sam,

First of all, I want you to know that I am sorry for keeping you so hidden—hidden from me and those I love. God's special and unique design of who I am is hidden in you, my true child self. I need you. I need you in order to be whole. I thought we would be better off if I just closed you off and shut you down. I was embarrassed by your feelings. I didn't understand that children just feel. I decided I didn't need feelings, but I was wrong. I know you felt helpless to defend yourself, so you turned to anger to scare off anyone who would shame you. I remember getting so mad and acting so mean to get others to leave me alone. But now I have been alone too long and I don't want to live like that anymore. My wife and my children are tired of my anger. We have learned to push away the very people we love the most. I lost so much when I abandoned you, and I am not willing to lose my family too.

I am sorry for being so harsh and ugly to you—the tender places in my heart. Will you forgive me for not loving and caring for you? I promise not to beat you down. I will let you have your rightful place inside of me so we can be one. I was not able to identify and process the emotions properly, so I did the only thing I knew to do to protect my soft heart—I created a hard shell around it. But that shell has kept others out of our lives and at arm's length. I have asked our Father to remove that shell and make us soft and pliable again. He is our defense now. We can just rest and learn to BE. I lay down all my efforts to have all the answers and defend myself. I see now that my angry, hard self was just a pointer to a little boy who was hurting and scared. I want you to know we can make it together. There is much I want to learn from you. If the Father says, "Come as a child," then I trust His Word and trust you to take me where I need to go to meet Him face-to-face. Thanks for coming back home.

I love you,

Sam (the adult)

Leaning on the Arm of Our Beloved

I (Denise) love the words in Hosea 2:14–15: "Therefore I am now going to allure her; I will lead her into the wilderness and speak tenderly to her. … [I] will make the Valley of Achor [achor is the Hebrew word for trouble] a door of hope."

In Song of Songs 8:5, the object of God's love comes forth in her true identity: "Who is this coming out of the wilderness, leaning [a position of dependence] on the arm of her beloved?"

Applying these words to us, we see the Lord in his unfathomable love making us dependent on him once again, as a child is dependent, by purposely alluring us into the wilderness. According to his plan and timing, he intends to transform our valleys of trouble—our heart wounds—into doorways of great hope.

PRAYER

Jesus, your ministry here on earth made a place for children. Your heart was, and still is, turned toward them. I invite you to show me more about the child within me. Is my own heart turned toward that child? Do I embrace this child like you do? Or would I rather, like your disciples, shoo the child away because there are more important things to attend to?

Do I, like a child, engage in the wonder and joy of your creation?

Jesus, you reveal your Father's heart. I want my heart to be in agreement with you and your Father about the child inside me. I want to be healed and whole—every part of me—and I invite you to reveal where this child was wounded and bring your healing love to those places.

Please also show me where my picture of you has been distorted, and help me to see you and your heart from a place of truth. By your grace, I will embrace my child within and bring that part of me to you. I trust you in this. In your name I pray, amen.

QUESTIONS FOR REFLECTION

1. Review the section, "Putting Away Childish Things." How would you describe the differences in being childlike versus being childish? Share a few everyday examples.

2. Which childlike qualities would you like to demonstrate in your adult life? Are there any childlike characteristics you would rather not incorporate into your life? Share your thoughts or feelings behind your selections.

3. Consider your answers to the section "Assessing Your View of Father God." Whether they are good, bad, or ugly, identify the applicable descriptions of how you saw your father and mother (or any other caregivers who fit either role) when you were growing up. How do you view God today?

4. Ponder this statement: "The biggest impact on how we see God is not our knowledge of the Scriptures, but the representation or misrepresentation of God that we saw mirrored in our parents." How true is this statement in your own life experience?

5. Slowly read and pray the closing prayer out loud. Ask Jesus to work it into your heart. Now take a deep breath and yield to his healing journey for you.

CHAPTER FOUR

WHAT DOES GOD FEEL— ABOUT US?

*I feel like I will be the lost lamb Jesus goes trudging
into the cold dark to find—when all the rest of the good
little flock is safely into the barn—only to have him
shake his head at me, pick me up with a sigh,
and wonder why he puts up with me. I wonder if there
was ever a point in my life where he looked at me with
pleasure, or was he always disappointed with me? Was
it something I did? Or just who I am?*
—*An abuse survivor sharing how she sees God*

One of the themes we see in counseling is our clients' personal lack of awareness of and connection with how God feels—not about their sins, or their failures, or even their successes, but about them.

About us.

About *you*.

Many whom we counsel will initially say that they know how God sees them. After all, the Bible makes it plain, right? Yet when we ask the questions, "How does the Father feel about you?" or "How did the Father feel when that happened to you?" they don't know what to say. They have never thought about how God *feels* when it comes to them personally.

Once again we see the great disconnect between what our head knows and our heart feels.

Does God Have Feelings?

Does God have feelings or emotions? While some may argue that God is not normally described in such terms, Scripture offers many examples to the contrary. For example, Jeremiah 31:3 states the following regarding the Lord's attitude toward his people: "I have loved you with an everlasting love; I have drawn you with loving-kindness." The Hebrew word for *love* in this passage is the same word that is used many times in the Old Testament. It means *to have a strong emotional attachment to and desire either to possess or to be in the presence of another.* It includes the love between a man and a woman as well as the love that a parent has for a child. It is more than a loving action—it is also the related feelings.

Again referring to God and his people, Israel, Isaiah 66:13 states, "As a mother comforts her child, so will I comfort you…." This Hebrew word for *comfort*, used many places in the Old Testament, means *the actions and feelings of comfort—such as consolation, reassurance, or encouragement—given from one to another.*

The New Testament furnishes many examples of Jesus expressing emotion. For instance, John 13:23 describes John as "the disciple whom Jesus loved." The word for *love* here does not refer to a loving action, but rather to Jesus's tender affection toward John.

In effect, the author of the book of John has described *himself* as the one whom Jesus loved. Think about that. What if we walked around saying the same thing about ourselves: "I'm the one whom Jesus loves." Some might think it prideful, but we would nevertheless be perfectly in line with how God feels about us!

As counselors, we might propose the above as a healing exercise, a memory verse for the day (for our whole life, actually): "I'm the one whom Jesus loves." It has a nice ring to it, doesn't it! What a wonderful change it would be from our usual self-talk.

Jesus displayed emotion dramatically right before he raised Lazarus from the dead. John 11:35 records the shortest verse in the Bible with the simple yet profound words, "Jesus wept."

Matthew 23:37 MSG records that Jesus lamented over—cried for, grieved over, bewailed—his own people, Israel. "Jerusalem! Jerusalem!" he cried. "Murderer of prophets! Killer of the ones who brought you God's news! How often I've ached to embrace your children, the way a hen gathers her chicks under her wings, and you wouldn't let me."

In the gospel of Mark 3:1–5 MSG, witness the intense ferocity of Jesus:

Then [Jesus] went back in the meeting place where he found a man with a crippled hand. The Pharisees had their eyes on Jesus to see if he would heal him, hoping to catch him in a Sabbath infraction. He said to the man with the crippled hand, "Stand here where we can see you." Then he spoke to the people: "What kind of action suits the Sabbath best? Doing good or doing evil? Helping people or leaving them helpless?" No one said a word. He looked them in the eye, one after another, *angry* now, *furious* at their hard-nosed religion. He said to the man, "Hold out your hand." He held it out—it was as good as new! (Italics added)

John 2:14–17 AMP tells of another time when Jesus's anger and indignation blazed forth in electrifying action. Furious with the money changers in the temple who were defiling his Father's house, he overturned their tables. "And His disciples remembered that it is written [in the Holy Scriptures], Zeal (the fervor of love) for Your house will eat Me up. [I will be consumed with jealousy for the honor of Your house.]"

Jesus also showed overt joy. When the seventy-two disciples he had sent on a "ministry trip" returned and excitedly shared their experiences with him, Luke 10:21 says that Jesus was filled with joy. The Greek root word for *joy* in this passage actually means *to jump for joy*. Some say that Jesus literally jumped up and spun around with delight. If we saw him show that much emotion today, it would undoubtedly make many of us uncomfortable. We might even tell him to tone it down!

Some clients have been able to relate to Jesus in his humanity but can't seem to see the Father in the same way. But Jesus's words to the apostle Philip in John 14:9 apply to us as well: "Anyone who has seen me has seen the Father." There it is, right before our eyes—more good news:

Anyone who has seen Jesus has also seen the Father.

Anyone who has seen Jesus in all his tenderness, gentleness, compassion, intense honesty, tenacity, righteous anger, grace, and love has seen the Father as well. Jesus perfectly mirrors the Father and is stamped with his very nature. Thus we can conclude that the feelings of Jesus's heart—the full range and depth of his emotions—faithfully and fully reflect the feelings of his Father's heart.

Why Is It Important to Know What God Feels?

You might be wondering, "Is it really all that important to know that the Father feels, and to know *what* He feels?"

Absolutely—it matters a great deal. For you to be able to say, "I know God loves me," is important. But to say, "I can feel his feelings of love for me," moves the fundamental truth of God's love for you into your heart.

For example, when we grieve over a significant loss, whether a loss from childhood or from today, if we can feel that the Father grieves with and for us, it draws us more deeply into his heart and opens the door for greater healing and intimacy with him. It makes the words in Psalm 34:18 even more meaningful: "When you are brokenhearted, I am close to you" (Paraphrase ours).

In John 17:23, Jesus said that the Father's love for us is the same as the love he has for Jesus. To know this is very important. But to also *feel* this love from the Father takes it to another level, a level we believe God desires for all of us.

Moreover, feeling the emotions of the Father, including his heart's cry that we turn our hearts to him, can motivate us in ways that otherwise wouldn't happen. According to Romans 2:4, it is the kindness and goodness of God that leads us to repentance—that is, change. However, if we are unable to feel his kindness and goodness toward us, then making whatever change he desires will be more difficult, even though it is for our own good. We will find ourselves relying on our own good intentions and suck-it-up willpower: what we should and ought to do in order to change. That approach leads nowhere. When God's kindness and tender support are left out of the picture, we experience temporary change at best and are ultimately doomed to fail in our own ability.

Breakthrough Moments of Healing

The healing of our hearts is more a journey than an event. However, Denise and I have experienced with our counselees, times when the Father breaks into our hearts. It can sometimes help to position ourselves for such breakthroughs. We cease from our busyness and allow our hearts to grow still enough to feel; or we find a quiet place to write to God; or we turn on some music and rest in a peaceful environment.

However, breakthrough moments often come when we least expect them and our guard is down.

I (Jerry) recall a number of these powerfully emotional moments several years ago when I was going through the deepest part of my healing journey. I remember one time specifically. Denise and I were living south of Houston, and we met after work at a theatre to see the movie *Field of Dreams*. On my way home, driving by myself, I wept so strongly that I almost had to pull over. The flood gates finally opened that evening, and my deep grief over my unmet needs for my earthly father's love, attention, and affection came pouring out.

I remember that breakthrough moment so clearly, though it happened long ago. That evening, in the midst of the pain, God did something in my heart that brought a healing salve to my wounds.

Donald Miller, in his book *Father Fiction*, shares how a breakthrough moment came for him:

…It was the week before Father's Day, and a few of my friends had told me they were planning large dinners or trips to be with their dads. Perhaps it was because I was operating on so little sleep following a trip I'd taken—or perhaps it was because Father's Day is a foreign concept to me, like celebrating relationships with aliens—but on a particular night, I felt my soul collapsing. I was struggling against a writing deadline and feeling, as I often do, that whatever book I write will only hit the world as a burden to its library. I wanted a father to walk through the door and tell me this wasn't true, that I was here on purpose and I had a purpose, and that a family and a father and even a world needed me to exist to make himself and themselves more happy. And it occurred to me, then, that a father was not going to walk through the door, that there would be no encouragement, there would be no voice of calm.… It occurred to me this would never, ever happen. For the first time in my life, I realized, deep down, I never had a dad.

I don't cry much, but on that night I did. I lost it. I shoved my computer aside and buried my head in my pillow like a child and sobbed. I sobbed for nearly an hour. I hate saying this because it sounds so weak, and I don't like dramatics, but I remember the night quite well, and there was no question something busted open.

Somebody said realizing we are broken is the beginning of healing. And for me, some of the healing began that night.[8]

Finding the Father and His Feelings in the Midst of Our Pain

One of the dilemmas in the healing process is this: We desperately need God to come into our places of woundedness and heal what was lost or damaged in our hearts. Yet those same wounds cause us to protect our hearts and our emotions from trusting others—especially God. You may have some very real, significant issues with God for allowing you to experience the abuse, neglect, and rejection. Why did he not rescue and protect you the way a father should have and God could have? It is not uncommon to work through these struggles with God in the healing process.

As we help our counselees deal with their image of God, we try to walk with each one into the heart of the Father and discover his goodness. He is good no matter what, even when we do not understand his ways.

For me (Jerry), one particularly important and intimate time with God came during the most intense period of my healing journey. There were other occasions when I had to wrestle with God concerning questions I had about my childhood. But what made this period of healing so powerful was being able to feel my Father's heart toward me. Every time I felt significant grief over events of my youth, I could feel *his* grief as well. His pain for me and my situation. His sorrow—yet, at the same time, his hope for my future. *I felt his feelings during that difficult stretch of my healing path*—and that is what motivated me to keep going.

This awareness of how God felt toward me surprised me at first, but I soon came to expect it. I knew he was with me and that what I was doing, pursuing healing, was what he wanted for me.

A Letter to Abba Father—Personalized

One very helpful tool that we use to help clients see the heart of Father God toward them is "The Father's Love Letter." This letter, developed by fatherheart.tv cofounder Barry Adams, is a compilation of Scriptures that communicate the love of God as our true Father. It has gone around the world in various formats and is now in at least ninety different languages.[9]

In addition to sharing this letter with our clients, we have modified it to express its truths from the perspective of the recipient talking to the Father rather than the Father talking to us. We call the result the "personalized version," and we share it with you here as our invitation to drink in and ponder the heart of Father God toward you. As you read this letter, pay particular attention to the expression of feelings that accompany many of the words and phrases.

Dear Abba,

I may not have always known you, but you have known everything about me (Psalm 139:1). You know when I sit down and when I rise up (Psalm 139:2). You are familiar with all my ways (Psalm 139:3). Even the very hairs on my head are numbered (Matthew 10:29–31). I was made in your image (Genesis 1:27)—and in you I live and move and have my being (Acts 17:28). For I am your offspring (Acts 17:28). You knew me even before I was conceived (Jeremiah 1:4–5). You chose me when you planned creation (Ephesians 1:11–12). I was not a mistake—for all my days are written in your book (Psalm 139:15–16). You determined the exact time of my birth and where I would live (Acts 17:26). I am fearfully and wonderfully made (Psalm 139:14). You knit me together in my mother's womb (Psalm 139:13)—and brought me forth on the day I was born (Psalm 71:6).

You have been misrepresented by those who don't know you (John 8:41-44). You are not distant and angry, but are the complete expression of love (1 John 4:16). It is your desire to lavish your love on me (1 John 3:1)—simply because I am your child and you are my Father (1 John 3:1). You offer me more than my earthly father ever could (Matthew 7:11)—for you are the perfect Father (Matthew 5:48). Every good gift that I receive comes from your hand (James 1:17)—for you are my provider and you meet all my needs (Matthew 6:31–33). Your plan for my future has always been filled with hope (Jeremiah 29:11)—because you love me with an everlasting love (Jeremiah 31:3). Your thoughts toward me are as countless as the sand on the seashore (Psalm 139:17–18)—and you rejoice over me with singing (Zephaniah 3:17). You will never stop doing good to me (Jeremiah 32:40)—for I am your treasured possession (Exodus 19:5). You desire to establish me with all your heart and all your soul (Jeremiah 32:41)—and you want to show me great and marvelous things (Jeremiah 33:3).

If I seek you with all my heart, I will find you (Deuteronomy 4:29). As I delight in you, you will give me the desires of my heart (Psalm 37:4)—for it is you who gave me those desires (Philippians 2:13). You are able to do more for me than I could possibly imagine (Ephesians 3:20)—for you are my greatest encourager (2 Thessalonians 2:16–17). You are also the Father who comforts me in all my troubles (2 Corinthians 1:3–4). When I am broken-hearted, you are close to me (Psalm 34:18). As a shepherd carries a lamb, you have carried me close to your heart (Isaiah 40:11). One day you will wipe away every tear from my eyes (Revelation 21:3–4)—and you will take away all the pain I have suffered on this earth (Revelation 21:3–4).

You are my Father, and you love me even as you love Your Son, Jesus (John 17:23)—for in Jesus, your love for me is revealed (John 17:26). He is the exact representation of your being (Hebrews 1:3). Jesus came to demonstrate that you are for me, not against me (Romans 8:31)—and to tell me that you are not counting my sins (2 Corinthians 5:18–19). Jesus died so that you and I could be reconciled (2 Corinthians 5:18–19). His death was the ultimate expression of your love for me (1 John 4:10). Father, you gave up everything you loved that you might gain my love

(Romans 8:31–32). If I receive the gift of your son Jesus, I receive you (1 John 2:23)—and nothing will ever separate me from your love again (Romans 8:38–39). When I come home, you'll throw the biggest party heaven has ever seen (Luke 15:7). You have always been Father and will always be Father (Ephesians 3:14–15). Your question to me is … "Will you be my child?" (John 1:12–13). You are waiting for me (Luke 15:11–32).

Love,

_____(Your Name)

As we share this letter with our clients, we also invite them to make note of any words or phrases that they find particularly difficult to receive as true for them personally. For example, the reference to the Father "throwing us the biggest party heaven has ever seen" when we come home (to his heart) is often difficult for many of our clients to accept. They "know it's true" because it is scriptural, and it "may be true for others." But they have a difficult time believing it—and definitely feeling it—for themselves. This is because many never felt celebrated by their parents as children, and thus they continue to struggle with this concept as an adult.

We invite you to read the letter again. As you proceed through each truth, ask yourself, "Do I really believe this for myself?" and, "Do I *feel* these things about the heart of the Father toward me?" In the places that are especially difficult for you to believe and receive, invite the Father to show you what it is that hinders you. A memory or feeling may come to you. Simply acknowledge the struggle and let the Father begin to bring his healing into that place in your heart.

But What about God's Wrath and Judgment?

Over the years, we have worked with many people who have placed their faith and trust in Jesus Christ. Yet the predominant position these believers hold in their hearts is that God does not look on them with favor or delight. They may know in their heads that he is love, but in their hearts they feel that God is often either angry or distant and uncaring. We have devoted a great deal of this book to bring forth the true, biblical nature of a loving God in order to contradict these distorted beliefs and reveal him for who he really is. If we are unable to believe that God truly loves us and feels affection for us, how will we be able to love ourselves, love others, and love him back in the way that he desires?

In fact, Scripture is clear that "we love because he first loved us" (1 John 4:19). When this love from God results in loving ourselves, and loving ourselves in turn results in loving others more, then reciprocating God's love back to him in gratitude comes naturally.

Yet in attempting to bring greater heart connection with the true nature of this loving God, we do not want to eliminate other aspects of him that are also biblical but can be difficult to reconcile with his love.

Look at the following Scriptures from the New Testament and consider what Jesus shares from his heart with those who will listen:

> Do not be amazed at this, for a time is coming when all who are in their graves will hear his voice and come out—those who have done good will rise to live, and those who have done evil will rise to be condemned. (John 5:28–29)

> But I tell you that men will have to give account on the day of judgment for every careless word they have spoken. For by your words you will be acquitted, and by your words you will be condemned. (Matthew 12:36–37)

> For the Son of Man is going to come in his Father's glory with his angels, and then he will reward (other versions have *repay*) each person according to what he has done. (Matthew 16:27)

> How dreadful it will be in those days for pregnant women and nursing mothers! There will be great distress in the land and wrath against this people. (Luke 21:23)

Whoever believes in the Son has eternal life, but whoever rejects the Son will not see life, for God's wrath remains on him. (John 3:36)

We know that when we see Jesus, we see the Father (John 14:9), and when we hear Jesus, we hear the Father. So these words spoken by Jesus also reflect the heart of God. We often share with our clients that we must "love what God loves and hate what he hates." Can the hard words Jesus spoke be reconciled with the loving words that comprise so much of Scripture and that we have shared in this book? Does it make sense that this loving God can also hate, when his basic essence or nature is love?

We believe the answer is an emphatic *yes*. Let's explore this topic more deeply.

Seeing God's Righteous Anger through Distorted Lenses

Due to vision problems that began when I was young, I (Jerry) have had to wear glasses throughout my life. Without them, I can't see anything clearly. But when I have them on, everything comes into focus.

Ironically, we can have corrected vision physically while our hearts remain out of focus due to things that have negatively affected us. For instance, because my father had anger issues when I was young, I learned incorrectly that anger was bad. When my father's wrath came out, its impact shaped me in ways I did not realize until many years later. Among its effects, it caused me to place the emotion of anger in a category all its own, with the label "Bad" written all over it. My view of anger was totally distorted and out of focus compared with God's view of anger.

Not until years later, in the midst of my healing process, did I begin to see that anger, although often used inappropriately, is in itself a necessary and godly emotion. Unfortunately, one of the costs of my distorted belief about anger was an inability to view God and his emotions correctly. Although I knew the truth in Scripture that "God is love," the overlay of my father image in my heart caused me to fear God and his potential displeasure and anger with me. This fear wasn't always foremost in my thinking; nevertheless, some of the most difficult times in my healing journey were stamped with a strong fear and anxiety regarding God.

That is *not* what Scripture means when it speaks of the "fear of the Lord" bringing wisdom, understanding, and other virtues. This fear brought me torment. Unless we allow God to reveal and then heal our distorted understanding of anger, we will have a difficult time embracing this important aspect of God's nature.

God's Wrath Reveals His Love

In Deuteronomy chapter 4, Moses is teaching the Israelites about what they need to do and not do as they prepare to cross over into the Promised Land. In verse 23, he instructs them to remember the covenant they have made with God and to not make an idol in the form of anything God has forbidden. Moses follows in verse 24 with the statement, "For the Lord your God is a consuming fire, a jealous God."

When people read this verse, what often comes to mind is that this "burning God" is a God filled with wrath and anger who will destroy everything that gets in his way. Yet the deeper meaning of this passage points to the intense desire within God's heart for us. It is true that this desire, this burning passion, will ultimately destroy whatever hinders or opposes love. But this fiery wrath flows from his deep desire and love for his people.

In his book *The Pleasures of Loving God*, Mike Bickle elaborates on the consuming fire of a jealous God and on his corresponding judgment:

> God's fire of judgment is an overflow, a sub-department of His fire of burning desire for His people. It is a manifestation of passion that removes everything that hinders love. Does sin hinder love? God will judge it in fiery passion to free His bride [us]. Do enemies assault the people of God? Judgment will come upon the devil and his forces as God is stirred with fiery passion to protect

His beloved. God will judge his enemies because of fiery love. His heart will be increasingly stirred with fiery jealousy, and He will strike His enemies to protect and avenge His bride.[10]

God's Wrath Is Different from Human Wrath

In *The Good and Beautiful God*, James Bryan Smith makes a distinction between God's wrath and human wrath, which is often expressed as reckless and irrational passion. He describes God's wrath as follows:

> [God's wrath] is a mindful, objective, rational response. It is actually an act of love. God is not indecisive when it comes to evil. God is fiercely and forcefully opposed to the things that destroy his precious people, which I am grateful for. It is a sign of God's love: "God's wrath must be understood in relation to His love. Wrath is not a permanent attribute of God. Whereas love and holiness are part of his essential nature, wrath is contingent upon human sin; if there were no sin, there would be no wrath."
>
> Wrath is a necessary reaction of a loving and holy God, a good and beautiful God, to evil. God's wrath is a *temporary and just verdict on sin and evil.*[11]

Godly Limits Speak of Love

Some of our clients' parents never established any limits or boundaries with them when they were growing up. Although this may have felt good at the time, it did not communicate love. Just the opposite. Healthy, godly boundaries from parent to child, combined with appropriate freedoms, tell the child that he or she is valued and important and that the parent cares enough to put certain limits in place. In the same way, through Scripture and the example of Jesus, God has provided us with limits or boundaries to live a life fully alive.

When we work through the hurts from childhood that have caused us to see God as an unjust parent, we are able to realize that his highest concern is not to punish, but rather to stand against those things that are hurtful to us. When we sin, it hurts us, and thus it hurts God. Why? Because he loves us. However, he doesn't shame us or use fear or guilt to get us to stop or to do better. It is his holy love—his passion for us and his passion against whatever hurts us—that leads us to change. This is what Romans 2:4 means when it says that God's kindness leads us toward genuine repentance. This loving, kind God is a passionate God, and he exhibits wrath against whatever hurts us, others, and ultimately his own heart.

Should We Fear God?

A section on the wrath of God needs to address the issue of fearing God. The topic confuses many Christians, since Scripture speaks of the fear of God as something to cultivate and esteem. For people who have struggled with fear since the fall of humanity in the Garden of Eden, this doesn't make much sense.

The solution to this dilemma again hinges on understanding the true meaning of the word *fear* and on deconstructing our own distorted concepts of authority. We need to distinguish between healthy, godly authority versus fear-based control and domination.

Abraham Joshua Heschel, in his book *God in Search of Man*, explains that the phrase "the fear of God" is derived from the Hebrew word *yirah*. He writes,

> The word has two meanings—fear and awe. There is the man who fears the Lord lest he be punished in his body, family, or in his possessions. Another man fears the Lord because he is afraid of punishment in the life to come. Both types are considered inferior in Jewish tradition. Job, who said, "Though he slay me, yet will I trust in him" (Job 13:15), was not motivated by fear but rather by awe, by the realization of the grandeur of eternal love.

Fear is the anticipation of evil or pain, as contrasted with hope which is the anticipation of good. Awe, on the other hand, is the sense of wonder and humility inspired by the sublime or felt in the presence of mystery…. Awe, unlike fear, does not make us shrink from the awe-inspiring object, but, on the contrary, draws us near to it. This is why awe is compatible with both love and joy. In a very real sense, awe is the antithesis of fear. To feel "The Lord is my light and my salvation" is to feel "Whom shall I fear?" (Ps. 27:1). "God is our refuge and strength. A very present help in trouble. Therefore we will not fear, even though the earth be removed, and though the mountains be carried into the midst of the sea" (Ps. 46:1–2).[12]

As I (Jerry) mentioned earlier, I struggled in the past with an unhealthy "fear of the Lord." It was a demonic, tormenting type of fear. I wasn't so much afraid that God was going to pour out his wrath upon me because I couldn't be good enough, clean enough, holy enough. Because I knew me. I knew my struggles and my sin, and I feared that these things would ultimately cause God to reject me. This was after I had given my heart to him and confessed my faith and trust in his Son, Jesus Christ. In my mind I knew what Scripture said about his heart for me, but in the deeper, wounded place of my feelings, my distorted beliefs caused me to operate in an unhealthy fear of God. Though I needed him desperately, this fear made it very difficult to draw near to him.

S.J. Hill, in his book *Enjoying God*, sums it up this way:

It is the awe and reverence of the Father that brings us close to His heart and leads us into a life of spiritual and emotional wholeness. Proverbs 14:26 tells us that "in the fear of the Lord there is strong confidence" (NKJV). We can rest assured that even when He disciplines and corrects us, He still enjoys us. Far too many Christians mistake divine correction for divine rejection. But the Father's correction is deeply rooted in His affection for us. Proverbs 3:11–12 admonishes us to "…not despise the Lord's discipline and do not resent his rebuke, because the Lord disciplines those he loves, as a father the son he delights in." While He may be displeased with a certain area in our lives, He is not displeased with us as a person.[13]

Because of the toxic shame that was still strong in me (Jerry), I couldn't make this distinction about the loving discipline of God the Father. I viewed anger, wrath, and fear as unloving and something to run from. Not until the lies in my core self began to be replaced by God's love and my heart began to heal could I begin to see these attributes of God as good. Once I did, I began to run *to* him and allow him to stand right with me, his arm around me. My sin and struggles were no longer all mine to iron out; now my Father and I worked on them together.

The Nature of the Father's Love: A Story

As we finish this chapter, let's look at another example of the nature of the Father's love for us from a father's perspective. In the following narrative, Donald Miller shares a conversation he had with a friend, John, whom he lived with for a while as a young adult. John was married to Terri at the time, and they had small children, including a boy named Chris.

John says to Donald,

> I don't know, Don, maybe you have to be a father to understand it. And I think someday you will understand it. But there isn't any love like this [the love of God as Father]. I love Chris and the girls in a way I can't explain. I really can't. It feels like some kind of miracle. I want them to love life; I want to give them joy; I want them to mature. And now that I have felt all this, I understand so much more of life; I understand why a sunset is beautiful; I understand why I don't get what I want all the time; I understand why God disciplines me; I understand God is a father.[14]

Later, Don continues the story:

He [John]told me that when Terri gave birth to Chris and he held his son in his arms for the first time, it was the closest he had ever been to understanding the love of God. He said that though he had never met this little person, this tiny baby, he felt incredible love for him, as though he would lie down in front of a train if he had to, that he would give up his life without so much as thinking about it, just because this child existed. …In other relationships, the person he knew had to earn his love. …But it wasn't that way with his children. His love for them was instantaneous, from the moment of their birth. They had performed nothing to earn his love other than be born. It was the truest, most unconditional love he had known. John said if his love for Chris was the tiniest inkling of how God loved us then he had all the security in the world in dealing with God, because he knew, firsthand, what God's love toward him felt like, that it was complete.[15]

We pray for this emotional connection with the Father's heart for every one of our counselees as they enter into their healing process. Sometimes this connection doesn't occur right away but may come later. We are all unique in our makeup and how God meets us on our healing paths. Whether you feel him strongly or not in the midst of your journey, rest assured that he indeed has feelings.

He has feelings of love for YOU.

And that's the truth.

PRAYER

Father, there is much that I need to know about you and your heart. I need to see you for who you truly are and let that revelation go deep into my very core. I desire to feel and function more from my heart and less from my head. I invite you to open my heart and begin to remove anything that hinders me from feeling those things that are in your heart for me. Your Son,

Jesus, lived from a passionate heart, and I want that as well. I believe you have made me in your image—feelings and all. Father, I want to feel what you feel, like Jesus, and be a reflection of that to others. I ask this in the name of your Son, Jesus, amen.

QUESTIONS FOR REFLECTION

1. How difficult would it be for you to tell the person next to you in church, "I am the one Jesus loves"? To emphasize the strength of affection John felt from Jesus, *The Message* translates John's reference to himself as "the one Jesus loved dearly" (John 13:22–25). Does this seem offensive or prideful to you on John's part to write about himself that way? Could you imagine that the Father would be delighted if you described yourself this way? Why or why not?

2. Ask yourself which of the following you believe and live from: "Nothing can separate me from the love of God," or (from the church marquee down the road), "Get Right or Get Left." Is there any difference in what you believe in your head versus your heart? Or do you hold a different standard for what you believe for others versus what you believe for yourself? Jerry shared that during his own healing journey, he could feel God's grief and sorrow for him over wounds that impacted his heart—yet at the same time, he could also feel God's hope for his future. Is the thought of feeling God's feelings for you, personally, a new revelation? How difficult is it for you to believe that God cares so much about you that he feels your sadness, despair, disappointment, and joy right along with you?

3. Reread "A Letter to Abba Father." Share the places where the words are especially difficult to believe and receive into your heart. Is this a familiar struggle from past hurts?

4. Picture this: You are the "one lost sheep" in Matthew 18:12–13. You are first on God's list. (In God's math, it is as if each one of us is the *only* lost sheep). You are not merely one of the ninety-nine. Your needs are important. Your wants. Your cries. Your tears. Your pain. Your shame. Your fear. Your hopes. Your dreams. Your identity. Your calling. Your destiny. All of these are important to God as well. Think on this for the next several days.

5.   Have you struggled with an unhealthy fear of the Lord? How do you respond to the following statement: God's fiery passion is against anything that hinders or opposes love—and it is centered on his love for you.

6.   Pray the closing prayer aloud from your heart. Father God will take you at your word—no striving required on your part.

CHAPTER FIVE

GOING BACK TO GO FORWARD

What negative emotions do I currently struggle with? Alone.
Bad. Guilty. Helpless. Hopeless. Inadequate. Inferior. Insecure.
Insignificant. Rejected. Self-condemning. Stupid. Unaccepted.
Unimportant. Worthless. I know I shouldn't feel this about
myself, but I can't keep these emotions from overcoming me.
—A pastor's daughter on her first appointment

The Journey of Going Home

We are convinced that true, spiritual healing ultimately will result in "coming home to the Father's house"—to his loving and healing heart. But in order for that to occur, we must be willing to journey back to our own house—that is, to the circumstances in which we grew up. Often, it is here where the Lord reveals how we were shaped by things that should not have happened to us but did, and by things that should have happened but did not. It is on this journey home that he shows us the things in our lives that align with his perfect plan and heals us from the things that were not. It is from this place that he allows us to find healing for our own hearts in order to find him.

One way to visualize this process is to think about a set of railroad tracks that symbolize the path God intended for us from the point we were placed on this earth. This set of tracks, designed by God, represents his perfect will for our lives. However, as we start out our lives and journey from that beginning point, we often begin to establish and travel on a different set of tracks which are not the ones he intended for us.

When we come to a place where we realize that we're on the wrong set of tracks, we have only one good choice: to stop, turn around, and allow God to take us back home, back to where we grew up, so we can find the healing we need along the way. Many of us would prefer to just jump the tracks at this point and move on with God's intended and better path. But this really isn't possible. God asks us to trust him and allow him to show us the areas of wounding in our hearts so we can forgive others, receive forgiveness for our own hurtful responses, and allow our Father to bring about true healing and restoration. The journey home is not easy, and it will take a while, but it is necessary.

As we take this train back to our homes of origin, the Father will point out signs and billboards of our past that we may or may not be aware of. We have to be willing to see whatever he wants us to see and feel whatever he wants us to feel. We need to be willing to see the truth about what happened to us growing up and how we responded to it, so we can begin to travel more in line with the path or the tracks that God truly intended for us.

Do you know where you are on this journey? Do you experience the Father's heart for you and for others? Can you be at rest in his house—in his heart? Does the fruit of your life indicate that maybe you veered off on a different set of tracks than the one God intended from the beginning? If so, he is asking you to stop and bring those parts of your heart back to him and allow him to heal you and establish you on the right path—his path.

What Every Child Needs and Deserves[16]

As we work with counselees, we ask them to reflect on different needs that we believe God says are important in our early developmental years, from birth to age seven. And we encourage them to ask themselves and the Holy Spirit, "To what degree did I receive these needs from my father and mother—to feel loved, to receive affection, to have a sense of belonging, to be protected, to be given a sense of freedom, to be given emotional guidance?" Let's unpack those needs.

To *feel loved* means that I felt special, precious, valued, important and significant—that I was deserving of the very best.

To have a *sense of belonging* means that I had a special place in the family. I made a special contribution; I occupied a position of importance.

To be given *protection* means that I knew my home was safe and free from harm. I could be myself. I was free to think and feel differently from others. I could have my own timing and ways of doing things and my own thoughts, feelings, and needs. And I could always feel assured of support and care.

To be given a *sense of freedom* means that I had the freedom to play and be spontaneous. I could laugh and explore and be creative. I could try new and different ways of doing things. I had my own sense of aliveness.

To be given *emotional guidance* means I was listened to and my thoughts and feelings were validated. I received the time and attention necessary to give me clear directions and help me solve problems. I felt coached and supported.

Many times when counselees look back at their childhood, they are unable to verify that enough of these important needs were met in their family. Their file is pretty empty.

Karen's Story

Karen, a young woman whom we were counseling, shared with us her experience of how her unmet childhood needs left a deficit in her heart, with costly consequences of self-contempt and self-hatred. Here is her story:

To Feel Loved: My dad never showed me that I was special, precious, valued or important. I was insignificant. I didn't matter. What mattered was how he felt and looked—how others perceived him and the family. I don't remember him telling me I was loved, or kissing me, or tucking me in, or reading to me. I thought he loved me because he supported our family nicely and, believe it or not, because he yelled at me. I thought his negative attention was better than no attention at all. I have many memories of being ridiculed, made fun of and yelled at in front of others. I have no memory of him showing love.

To Receive Affection: I was never touched or held by my dad, in fact he taught me the opposite. If mom touched me or him affectionately, he would make fun of it as a weakness and as "yucky." There are no pictures of him holding me or touching me. I learned that affection was not warm and positive, but weak and uncomfortable.

To Have a Sense of Belonging: I never had a place in the family. I was more like a pain in the ass. I never felt comfortable or safe with dad and mom. I hated being in the house and loved to go outside to get away by myself. At other times I stayed in my room alone. I felt safer and less tense there. I learned to walk around on eggshells and often felt scared that my dad would find something to ridicule and bully me for. I couldn't be myself around my dad because he would badger me until I agreed with him, so I always agreed with him because I wanted to avoid any conflict or battle.

Recently Karen felt the tender love of Father God for the little girl inside her. For the first time, she really felt valuable to God. She asked the Father to forgive her for hating herself and agreed with him to love what he loves. When our heart and spirit are wounded this deeply in our for-mative years, we need more than a Band-Aid. We need the Healer.

The Impact of the Father Wound

As discussed previously, the role of the father and the mother in a child's life is huge. Dad and mom are instrumental either in establishing a solid foundation for the child to move forward in healthy emotional and spiritual development, or in severely hindering that process. And contrary to what is often believed, some of the most severe emotional impact on a child and future-adult is not just from abusive actions, *but from the absence of loving actions.*

Studies have shown that there is more emotional damage to the devel-oping child from the "silent father" than from any other type, with the exception of the sexually-abusive father.[17] The silent father is passively rather than overtly destructive. Rather than bruises and scars on a child's outside, the bruises are all on the inside. As far as anyone can see, nothing has really been done to the child to account for the damage. The adult may even say, "I had a good childhood." But Dad's silence and uninvolvement foster dis-torted perceptions in a child. When there is a problem, the child concludes, "There must be something wrong with me. I must be the problem."

We mentioned earlier that one of the greatest needs in children is to know deep in their hearts that they belong—that their existence mat-ters. Donald Miller, in his book *Father Fiction*, describes how his father's leaving when he was very young impacted him in this area of belonging: (Note: Donald grew up with a working mom and his younger sister.)

> …I never thought to ascribe my mother's emotional and physical exhaustion to the lack of a husband and father; rather, I ascribed it to my existence. In other words, I grew up learning … that if I didn't exist, the family would be better off. I grew up believ-ing that if I had never been born, things would be easier for the people I loved.

A thought like this can cripple a kid…If a kid grows up feeling he is burdening the people around him, he is going to operate as though the world doesn't want him. I didn't recognize this feeling in myself the last few years—until my late twenties and early thirties—but it has always been there.[18]

Sometimes counselees have difficulty connecting with the pain of childhood memories because their parents are different now. But it does not matter how our parents treat us today as adults, because the shaping experiences happened to us when we were children. Although it is a good thing when parents become more mellow or supportive of us as adults, their doing so does not heal deep wounds that occurred in our formative years.

In my (Denise's) childhood, I never remember my dad telling me he loved me. Because I didn't hear the actual words, I had to learn that he loved me in other ways. He always provided for the family. *He must love me.* He sometimes took me to work with him. *He must love me.* He brought me a puppy. *He must love me.* (In retrospect, I think he got the puppy for himself, but the only way my mother would let him keep it was if it looked like a gift for me.)

Then, surprisingly, on my wedding day, when I was twenty years old, Dad told me for the first time that he loved me. I remember exactly where I was standing at the reception and all the commotion going on around me when he said those three words: "I love you." Obviously, they impacted me and left an imprint on my mind and heart, and it was wonderful to hear them. But they did not touch the empty places in my little-girl heart—the child within me who needed to know she was precious and special and loved and important to her father.

Roland Warren, president of the National Fatherhood Initiative, says it best: "Kids have a hole in their soul in the shape of their dads [and moms]. If a dad [or mom] is unable or unwilling to fill that hole, it leaves a void—it leaves a wound."[19] In ministry we have found only one way to heal this wound: inviting the Father who holds all time to go back in our lives and heal our broken hearts, filling places that are totally or partially empty and removing any taint of pain or shame or fear.

Returning to Donald Miller's story, he shares,

> ...as I've processed the ramifications of growing up without a father, I've realized the incredible hole in my heart this absence has left. I wish my father and I had a friendship and that he would call once every couple weeks and tell me I was doing a good job. I hunger for this. I don't actually like thinking about this stuff, but I have a sense *wounds don't heal until you feel them.* ... [I have to] come to the difficult truth that the pain is there because I wanted to be loved, and I wasn't. I wanted to be important to my father, but I wasn't. I wanted to be guided, but I wasn't. And then, honestly, [I have to be willing] to feel whatever it is that this hard truth creates—to respond in the way I need to respond.[20] (Emphasis added)

Here is a tragic letter that addresses the power of fatherlessness in a young girl's life:

Daddy,

Zero—nothing—0—nothing.
That's what you gave me.
That is what we have together as father and daughter.
NOTHING ...
I wanted a daddy so badly.
I just wanted what every little girl wants.
It's sad how much we both lost.
The really sad thing is that I feel like you had so much potential to be the best daddy ever.
What happened to you that you couldn't make that happen?
It is so sad your woundedness and weakness got in the way.

I wish you would have been strong enough to protect us from mom.

You couldn't even do that for yourself, so I guess you couldn't do it for me.

That makes me sad and angry.

You left me with nothing except a great big love hole in my heart.

You know what, Daddy?—If you would have been able to see me and hear me—

You would have realized what a sweet loving little girl I was.

How much I wanted and needed you to love me.

How much I wanted to please you and love you back.

A daddy is supposed to be a little girl's first love.

To show her what she is worth and how she should be loved.

You gave me none of that.

I have lived my whole life with a starving heart, getting nothing.

It is crushingly painful every day.

I know you actually did have something to give me.

That fact might even make it more painful.

But sadly enough for both of us, you couldn't figure out a way to give it.

I choose to forgive you, Daddy,

Even though I wish it was different.

I choose to forgive you, Daddy,

Even though I know it never will be.

I choose to forgive you, Daddy,

Even though it has cost me my very self.

—Your lost little girl

Mother Issues

As vital as the father is in the development of a child, the mother is equally important in different ways. It is the mother who nurtures the new life in her womb, and who continues that nurturance to the newborn and on into the first year or two of the child's life. During that first year, the child mirrors the mother and is an extension of her and the nurture she provides. In this very early period, the baby does not even realize that he is separate from his mother. Only when the father comes in and begins to draw the child away from the mother, ideally around age two or three, does the toddler become aware that he exists apart from his mother.

In this early period of the child's life, the mother is crucial in establishing the foundation of trust and security upon which the healthy development of the child can proceed. This foundational love is communicated in three main ways from the mother:[21]

Affectionate Touch. We were created for affection. Doctors have scientifically proven that without touch, the body and emotions become unhealthy. Touching someone says to them that they are important to you; they belong and they have value. If we did not receive affectionate touch in the right way as a child, then in our teenage years we may allow ourselves to be touched in the wrong way.

Eye Contact. The eyes are indeed the windows of the soul through which love is communicated to a child. They drink in the love that flows to them from eye contact with their parents. If children don't see understanding and loving looks in the eyes of their parents, a wound can result that remains unhealed all through life. A child may then may feel awkward, insecure, separate, and out of place in his or her relationships.

Tone of Voice. Babies learn to bond and trust when their parents look them in the eye and speak loving words in an encouraging, gentle, tender, and empathizing voice. The influence of mom and dad's voices continues all through a child's formative years. Loving tones nurture the soul and help children feel acceptance and value so they can walk free of the fear of rejection and failure.

When the mother is unable, for whatever reason, to effectively convey nurturance and love to the child through touch, eye contact, and voice, a breach can occur in the child's ability to trust and to rest in the mother's love and care. As a result, emotional abandonment, rejection, and a generalized insecurity often take root. Although these issues are not solely related to the mother, her role in them is extremely important.

We have seen many men and women trace the roots of such problems back to their relationship with their mothers. In some cases, the mother's fear of intimacy from her own deep wounds prevented her heart from being fully available to her little one. The child's heart and spirit did not receive what they needed to establish security and trust.

In other cases, the mother appeared to provide a great deal of nurturance and love; however, her own deep needs caused her to smother her child with "love" out of a need to feel valued, needed, and loved herself. In such instances, the mother is getting more than the child, who is left with empty places that will cry out to be filled later in life.

There are, of course, other more overt examples of harmful mother issues, such as physical absence; alcohol or other addictions; neglect of the child's basic needs; verbal, emotional, physical or sexual abuse; failure to protect the child from the abuse of others; or simply not being emotionally present. When mother issues such as these occur, a major crack results in the foundation of the child and future-adult.

The "Mother Heart" of a Nurturing God

God is neither male nor female. When we use the term *mother heart* to describe him, we are attempting to describe his personality—his very nature. Because we commonly refer to God as Father, we may find it difficult to think about God as having a "mother's heart." Yet we know that God created us in his own image, and he said that he created us male and female (Genesis 1:27). So if we're male and female and made in his image, then his nature must include both masculine and feminine characteristics.

Various Scriptures refer to this type of nurturing love of God. Here are a few of them:

Can a mother forget the baby at her breast and have no compassion on the child she has borne? Though she may forget, I will not forget you! See, I have engraved you on the palms of my hands. (Isaiah 49:15–16)

I have loved you with an everlasting love; I have drawn you with loving-kindness. (Jeremiah 31:3)

Before I formed you in the womb I knew you, before you were born I set you apart. (Jeremiah 1:5)

Here is one of the strongest expressions of God's nurturing mother heart:

For you will nurse and be satisfied at her comforting breasts; you will drink deeply and delight in her overflowing abundance. For this is what the Lord says: "I will extend peace to her like a river, and the wealth of nations like a flooding stream; you will nurse and be carried on her arm and dandled on her knees. As a mother comforts her child, so will I comfort you; and you will be comforted over Jerusalem." (Isaiah 66:11–13)

This is the God who desires to heal us. He is the One who created in us the need for a deep, foundational nurturing love, and he *will* heal all our wounds—including our mother wounds—and reestablish our areas of broken trust.

When a Child Parents a Parent

Sometimes the role of the child gets confused because of the unmet needs of a parent. Most commonly, the child takes on a caretaker responsibility for nurturing or protecting that parent instead of receiving nurture and protection. The child hopes to make up for the parent's hurt, pain, loneliness, or unhappiness, especially in the marriage, by trying to please that parent and keep the peace.

A child in this position does not learn to identify and value her own needs, feelings, and identity. She loses childlikeness early on and becomes more adult-like as she learns to carry the burdens of others. She is often applauded for her "grownup behavior," for being so responsible and so "good." No one notices that she is not being allowed to be a child. There is no time for that since she is too busy taking responsibility for others.

Anna learned that it was up to her to keep her dad happy. She would let Dad win when they played board games together. That way she avoided getting an angry outburst from him, since he was competitive and a poor loser. He especially didn't want to lose to a child.

Dad expected Anna to spend Saturdays with him, even though she wanted to go play outside with her friends. Sometimes he wouldn't speak to her for days because she didn't run and say hi to him when he came home. He needed her to give him what he needed and wanted, since his wife was not emotionally or relationally available to him.

Like Anna, Terry also learned to be responsible for a parent. Terry's parents were miserable in their marriage, and the emotional connection between them was nonexistent. Both Dad and Mom *n-e-e-d-e-d* the children to make their lives tolerable. Terry felt overwhelming guilt if he didn't say goodnight to his parents. He remembers going into his parents' bedroom and tucking his dad in at night, often cuddling up and sleeping next to him until his mom came to bed a couple of hours later.

This continued into his teen years, with Terry trying to meet his parents' needs while also seeking to fill a hole in his own heart for affection and love that never made it in. It didn't help that Dad's favorite was his sister. Terry's dad attached to her when she was very young and made her his emotional confidante. Terry's mom, on the other hand, became enmeshed with Terry and was excessively possessive of him; it was as if he wore a tee shirt that said, "He's mine!" Strangely, his mom was not affectionate toward him and never hugged him, kissed him, or told him that she loved him. She just needed him for herself.

Although Terry is now a married adult and on his own, his mother still calls him her "precious baby" and buys things just for him. She counts the days until she can see him again. This is NOT OKAY for Terry or his wife or their marriage relationship. Terry has tried to "leave and cleave" from his parents, but his mother won't let go.

A Personal Story of Love Going the Wrong Way

I (Jerry) experienced a significant mother wound as a child. However, not until my mid-thirties did I become aware of it, thanks to the insight of a pastoral counselor.

I had always known of my father's workaholic behavior and his issue with impatience, anger, and rage. Even as a young adult, I sensed that growing up in that environment had affected me. I had struggled with fear and anxiety for some time, and I attributed a good part of it to my father.

Much to my shock, however, when my counselor heard my story during our first appointment, he had another opinion. "Jerry, I agree that your father has significantly affected you," he said, "and yes, it will be important to address this matter during your healing process. However, I believe that the bigger issue for you is dealing with the impact of your mother when you were growing up."

I looked at him with a confused, deer-in-headlights expression. "Is this guy crazy?" I thought. "Maybe this will be my first and last appointment with this counselor." There wasn't time for him to elaborate on why he had reached his conclusion, especially since he had only heard a twenty-to-thirty-minute account of my childhood and my current, besetting issues. But something inside me sensed that the man was onto something. As I continued counseling with him, I discovered that his conclusion was right on, and I am so grateful for his insight.

Let me provide a little more background. Because of my father's unhealed issues, he was unable to deal effectively with his inner pain. The predominant emotion he expressed was anger. That anger pointed to various other issues, such as fear and anxiety and a deep need to succeed and avoid the shame of not measuring up. These issues, fueled by financial stressors, created tension between my father and my mother, whose needs for greater emotional intimacy in her marriage were not being met.

I was the youngest of three sons, having come along four years after my brother before me, and for whatever reason, I adopted the role of my mother's emotional caretaker. When she cried, I tried to comfort her. When she and my father argued, I attempted to get in the middle to protect her emotionally. During the times when my mother felt especially hurt and frustrated with my father, she would share her thoughts and feelings with me.

Although my mother did not realize it, she was getting a significant amount of her emotional needs met through me.

So as I met with my counselor that first session and he confronted me with having mother issues, all I could think in response was that my mother had been the one who was emotionally present for me and my siblings. Having mother issues just didn't make sense.

Yet in the months ahead, I came to understand that much of the love and nurture my mother showed me as a child did not meet my emotional needs. Rather, the attention she gave me was an attempt to fill her own unmet needs. Much of her love was *going in the wrong direction*. As a result, I came away with a love deficit. The unhealthy closeness between my mother and me resulted in significant struggles in the early years of my marriage with Denise.

We have worked with many men and women who as children lost their childhood by assuming responsibility for one or both parents. As these clients have become aware of how an inordinately close parent connection affected them, they have experienced the Father's healing touch for this core identity issue.

When Memories Are Missing

Many who come to us struggle with anger, rage, depression, anxiety, loss of purpose and calling, relational conflict, or addictions of various types. They often also find it hard to connect with God on an intimate level. Yet when they reflect on their early developmental years—the period when their identity is shaped—they cannot identify any specific negative memories that could have caused their current struggles. Some individuals have very few memories at all from their first six or seven years of life.

For this reason, many people disregard the possible connection between their problem and their childhood experiences. When these persons enter into a process of unpacking their baggage from childhood, their bags appear to be empty. Thus, one of the most important issues for many counselees has, in our experience, also been among the most frequently overlooked.

When the needs of a child go unmet—needs that God designed to be met by the child's primary caregivers—significant consequences arise in later years. This kind of wounding can be as damaging as some more overt wounds, although it is more difficult for the person to identify. A healing-of-memories approach often does not work as well in such cases.

Maybe, during a church service, you went forward for healing prayer for emotional struggles and did not find much help. Yet you know of someone else who also received prayer and received significant healing for a memory which surfaced at that time. Such experiences can result in a great deal of shame and self-condemnation. We wonder, "What's wrong with me? Why doesn't God heal me?" You need to know there's nothing wrong with you. Sometimes there simply are no specific memories that need to be healed, and thus the healing needs to come in a different way.

We Parent Ourselves the Way We Were Parented

People learn to shame themselves and parent themselves the same way they were parented. Denise and I see this reality proven time and again in counseling. Let us ask you a question:

> Would it be okay with you if your son or daughter grew up in your place in your home of origin? You could be a fly on the wall and watch, but you couldn't intervene in any way—you could only observe.

> Your son or daughter would grow up in exactly the same circumstances as you, getting the same treatment from your parents, siblings, and grandparents.

> Would that be alright with you?

When we ask this question during counseling, something powerful often happens in the counselee. All the pretending, all the fantasy, all the loyalty to family (especially toward parents), and all the minimizing of damage hit the fan of God's truth. The person is forced to confront all of the devices they have used to avoid feeling the pain buried inside.

He or she may have convinced themselves that "it wasn't that bad—other kids had it worse."

He may have persuaded himself that "my parents loved me even though they didn't show it or say it."

She may voice common statements: "They did the best they could." "They had a rough childhood too."

But these common beliefs often crumble quickly when the counselee responds strongly with, "No, it would *not* be alright if my child grew up in my place in my home of origin." The person is often surprised to find their response accompanied by tears running down their face. When this happens, we stop, lean forward, and emphatically say, "That's the Father's heart: These surprising emotions. The tears. That's the Father's heart—for *you*."

This response by the client reveals two standards in operation. One is the standard he applies to himself; the other is the standard he uses for others. Such double-standards are never in agreement with the Father's heart.

We strive to parent our own children well; yet we may continue to parent ourselves the way we were parented, harshly and critically. But what if God said to you right now, "My child, I asked your parents to give you more than you received"? What about that?

Can you make up excuses for your parents when God says that you needed more quality time with your dad instead of seeing the back of his newspaper or him on his computer? That you needed hugs at bedtime and words like, "You are special and we are proud of you"?

And what if there were some things you never should have received from your parents, like a slap across your face, or welts on your bottom, or shaming words like, "You'll never amount to anything," or, "Shame on you"?

Over the years we have heard many painful stories of words that have wounded fragile child hearts:

"You're not worth the gun powder to blow you to hell."

"I never wanted a split-crotch (a girl)."

"The only reason we adopted you is because nobody else would take you."

"Your father wanted you when you were born, but by the time you were two, he was disappointed he ever had you."

"Get it right or get the belt."

"You're a disappointment and you're going to hell."

"You're no better than a mutt on the street."

"You look like a whore."

And how about this one: after a terrific last-second basketball play, your dad says after the game, "You almost missed. That was your only good play all day."

The lies of critical self-talk ride in on the arrows of such words. But it is not only spoken words that can pierce a child's heart. A critical look, a harsh gesture, or just being ignored all can teach a child that he is inadequate, unloved, unwanted, worthless, and unimportant.

Growing up under such loveless parenting puts us at a distinct disadvantage when we turn our lives over to God. We want God to love us, but we judge ourselves lacking and pathetic and disqualified.

Still, the Father asks us to love what he loves. If we hate what God absolutely loves and cherishes, we will continue to struggle to find his heart. God's heart and the feelings that flow from it are critical to *knowing* him.

PRAYER

Lord Jesus, I desire to live fully alive, with the fruits of the Spirit—love, joy, and peace—active in my life. I know there are things that are affecting me and preventing me from living fully from this place. I am willing to go back in order to go forward, and I invite you to show me anything that is necessary for me to see and deal with in order for healing to occur.

I cannot know these things unless you reveal them to me, and I know that you reveal what you plan to heal. Thank you for loving me enough to take me back to the home I grew up in, so that I can truly rest in the home you have prepared for me: your heart. In your name I pray, amen.

QUESTIONS FOR REFLECTION

1. How would you describe where you are presently in your healing journey? Do you experience the Father's heart for you and for others? Can you be at rest in his house, that is, his heart? In what ways does the fruit of your life indicate that you may have veered onto a different set of tracks from what God intended for you at the beginning? If so, he is asking you to stop and bring those parts of your heart back to him and allow him to heal you and establish you on the right path—his path.

2. Review the section "What Every Child Needs and Deserves." To what degree would you say your father met each of the needs described in the list? How about your mother? Consider your emotional struggles as you ponder this question: How do you think the manner in which your parents met or failed to meet your needs as a child has impacted your life? The following words may help you identify some of your feelings: alone, bad, guilty, helpless, hopeless, inadequate, inferior, insecure, insignificant, rejected, self-condemning, stupid, unaccepted, unimportant, worthless.

3. Consider these wise counseling sayings: You can't heal what you don't feel. Feel it to heal it. Grieve it to leave it. What God reveals, he plans to heal. How have these sayings been experienced in your life?

4. When you look back on your childhood, what abusive actions have wounded you? What wounding have you experienced from the *absence* of loving actions?

5. Review the section "When a Child Parents a Parent." Is this applicable to you? How so?

6. MIRROR EXERCISE
   Standing in front of a mirror, look directly and deeply into your own eyes and speak the following affirmations. They are truths that agree with how God our Father feels toward you, truths that make him smile. Speaking them will feel awkward at first, but repeat this exercise daily until you believe it.

I love you, _____ (your name).

I am fearfully and wonderfully made.

I am a precious treasure to God.

I am the one Jesus loves dearly.

I am the apple of God's eye, and he celebrates the day I was born.

I was on his mind from the beginning of time.

He calls me by name— _____ —and says, "You are mine."

There is nothing I could ever do to make him love me more.

There is nothing I could ever do to make him love me less.

I am special.

I am a daughter/son of the King.

I am a treasure and a delight.

God loves _____ and I love you.

7. Read the closing prayer aloud. Add to it your own hopes and desires for this healing journey.

FOUNDATIONAL BUILDING BLOCKS: TRUST AND IDENTITY

A part of you was left behind very early in your life:
the part that never felt completely received. You want yourself
to be one. So you have to bring home the part of you that was
left behind. When you befriend your true self and discover
that it is good and beautiful, you will see Jesus there.
Where you are most human, most yourself, weakest, there Jesus
lives. Bringing your fearful self home is bringing Jesus home.
—Henri Nouwen

The Earliest Building Block: Trust

Did you know that the first and most foundational building block of your entire life is trust? And that trust is formed in the first nine months after your birth? And that all the other building blocks such as independence, identity, confidence, and initiative are built on trust?

Did you know that trust is the foundation for all relationships, and therefore a break of trust in the first year of life causes a break all the way through life? Did you know that when such a breach of trust occurs, the greatest loss is that you cannot hold your heart open to love, whether it is love for God or self or others?

Basic trust lies at the core of self-confidence and freedom from what others think. Trusting in who you are as a valued human being safeguards you from being easily manipulated and controlled by others, so you don't lose track of who you are or become a non-person. A strong foundation of trust provides you with the freedom to entrust your heart to others and to God.

If you grow up with a breach in this foundational building block in the first year of your life, you will often struggle with fear and anxiety; with performing or people-pleasing for love and acceptance; with being either excessively compliant or dominant and controlling; or with difficulty in adapting to change.

To get at the root of these issues and to the core pain surrounding them, we often ask our counselees several questions:

- How long have you felt this anxiety around others or even when you are alone?
- How long have you felt that something was wrong with you?
- How long have you felt responsible for everyone and everything?
- How long have you felt you were a burden, a mistake, shortchanged, unknown for who you really are?
- How long have you felt you were a non-person?

When the answer is, "for as long as I can remember," then we know that the heart was damaged very early in life—even before memories form, which is prior to age three.

As you consider your inner child, remember that children are not just short adults. They are kids. They are small. They don't think like you think as a grownup. They are immature; they don't have your education or experience. A child has no way of understanding that when a parent withholds love or affirmation or affection or belonging, or when a caregiver afflicts the child with verbal, emotional, physical, or sexual abuse, such behavior reflects something sadly missing in the adult, not something hopelessly flawed in the child.

Did you get that? It wasn't your fault.

Your parents missed the mark, not you.

And you always thought something was wrong with you.

With clients who have, for example, been sexually violated by a family member, we often find it helpful to have them think of a child they know who is the same age that the client was when the abuse occurred. The child may be a niece or nephew. It may be their own little boy or girl, or their grandchild, or a child next door, or one they saw at church or in the grocery store earlier in the day. The point of the exercise is to help the counselee see how much that child is a *child*.

Would you even question the fact that God asks the adult to parent the vulnerable, impressionable, naive, dependent baby, toddler, child, youth, adolescent, and teen? You were supposed to be a child growing up—*not* a responsible adult from the beginning.

As counselors, we are awestruck when we see the Father heal all of the wounded parts in people of all different ages. Because God always was, and is, and is to come, he can go back in time when we can't. Time doesn't constrain him; he can be in the past, present, and future all at the same time.

We need to spend time inviting God to go back into our inner child (our true, core self) to heal the broken places—because in Jesus, God came to heal the brokenhearted and set the captives free. And when God heals a broken heart, a life is transformed from the inside out.

My Puppy Experience

It was a hot Saturday morning where we lived south of Houston, and I (Jerry) was heading to our garage to prepare to cut the grass. Our garage was separate from the house, and I had already gone out and opened the door a few minutes earlier. When I entered the garage at this time, I heard a whimpering coming from under one of our cars. Crouching down to look, I saw a small dog way up toward the front of the car. He was terrified, shaking visibly and even urinating from his extreme fear. When I tried to draw closer to him, he recoiled. I needed to move the car out of the garage, but I didn't want to take a chance of hurting him—though actually, I was more concerned about alleviating some of his fear.

I got a small dish, filled it with cold water, and placed it near him. Since he wouldn't let me get close, I set the water as near to him as I could and began to talk quietly to him, encouraging him with the tone of my voice that he was in a safe place. He didn't have to be afraid any longer.

After about twenty minutes of this quiet encouragement, the pup got up enough nerve to come to the dish and take a drink. His fear appeared to subside, and he cautiously emerged from under the car and let me pet him. A few minutes later, he began to follow me up and down the sidewalk between our garage and house, sticking close to my feet. Shortly after, still by my feet, he began to jump around like a totally different dog from what I had seen thirty minutes earlier.

I was amazed. But what happened next was even more astonishing to me. A large dog entered our yard, and this rejuvenated little pup a quarter the size of the intruder proceeded to chase him away from me and out of our yard!

Within a half-hour, this little dog had moved from paralyzed fear to warrior and protector status—all from a few comforting words and a cup of cold water.

I stopped and began to cry because I sensed the power of God on me. His Spirit was telling me that what I had just witnessed was analogous to the Father's love for his children. I was crying because, in a vivid way, the Father had dramatized his love for me. I realized that in many ways I was that little dog, fearful to come out of hiding. I was afraid of how my heavenly Father would view me if he saw all of me, especially my sin and my shame.

Could I trust him? My mind knew of his love and goodness through the Scriptures I had read, but the revelation was not imprinted in my heart. To come out of hiding and into the light of his presence required a great risk on my part—risk of being hurt, or worse yet, risk that the Father would not approve of me, that I might not be acceptable to him. Through this "puppy experience," I saw that the Father not only wants us to come out of hiding, but he is wooing us to himself.

Why do we so often hide in fear rather than come out and run to the Father? There are many reasons, and most stem from early and sometimes repeated wounding to our spirits from significant people in our lives.

After my encounter with the little dog, I spoke with a neighbor about him. The neighbor said that earlier that morning, he had seen the same dog being beaten with a broom by its owner a couple houses down from ours. That filled in still more parts of the picture for me. Trust had gotten shattered—a problem we see so often in our counseling.

When we do not trust, we develop alternative ways of relating to each other and especially to the Father. We withhold a portion of our hearts and are unable to receive and give fully, the way God intended. The cure is to feel the Father's love for us and know that it is real and personal.

The Next Critical Building Block: Identity

Another profound developmental stage in children occurs between the ages of two and four. At this stage, we make one of the most impactful decisions in our entire life. It is an internal choice. Stated simply, it is,

"I am me and I'm OKAY."

or

"I am me and I am NOT OKAY."

Which choice did you make? You don't have to search very long to determine which one it is. Often, taking a quick look at your self-talk gives you the clues you need.

If "I am me and I am okay," then I have the freedom to be different from you. I have the courage to say no. I can be separated from others and still feel safe. I know that I am the very apple of God's eye. I am me and I am special.

On the other hand, if "I am me and I am *not* okay," then I will learn to put on a false self and pretend to be whom I think you want me to be. I cannot say no because I do not want to offend you or risk your rejection.

I am certain that if you saw the real me, you wouldn't like me—because at my core, I don't like me either.

Let us interject a letter that a client wrote to his four-year-old inner child. It makes what we have shared about trust and identity more personal.

Dear little boy,

I have a feeling you were very well taken care of physically but that you probably did not have the emotional side of your needs met. When you were a baby, did you cry to be held and nurtured, but instead were just misunderstood? Did you as a little boy want to express your emotions but instead were rejected or made to feel that emotions were not important in your family? Did you feel the need to cry but did not feel the freedom to do so? Did you want your father to hold you, affirm you and play with you—but instead saw him walk by and not notice you—or maybe he wasn't even there for you at all? Did you go to your mother just to be held and cuddled and end up receiving her coldness—never being able to fill those desperate needs you had for touch?

I remember all the times you laid on your bed holding your teddy bear, Grizzle, crying that no one loved you but your bear. I wish I could have been there to hold you, just because I wanted to—to not let you go until you were done crying—to allow you to play and laugh and just be. I would have allowed you to let out the feelings you had in your heart but were never allowed to express in your home. I see you playing alone again and my heart hurts for you. I wish I could have been there to see exactly what you saw and feel exactly what you felt. I wish I could have helped you understand and be able to share your feelings and needs.

I would love to get to know you better and allow both our hearts to come alive. I met the Father who wants to father us both way better than any parents ever could. I know that's hard to believe but I am coming to realize He loves us real special. Did you know He calls us His favorite one? I want you to take hold of my hand and come with me. Let's both let the Father love on us and heal us. Then He will show us what's really in our hearts and what He really created us for.

Will you come with me? I see your blue eyes look at me and see the hope in your smile. Well then, what are we waiting for? Let's go!

The adult "boy"

My Fears as a Child

When I (Denise) was six years old, I had tremendous fears of abandonment, of separation, and of losing a loved one, especially my mother. I tried to keep my little world under control and became hyper vigilant of my surroundings—always wanting to make sure everything and everyone was okay. My internal prayer was that my family would "just love each other," and I remember praying often so that nothing bad would happen.

I don't think anyone in my family knows this, but when my mother took a nap in the afternoon (she worked the midnight shift), I watched over her to make sure she was breathing. When I wasn't certain, I ran and got a mirror and stuck it under her nose to see if her breath would fog it up. That's pretty bad. What a scared little girl!

Assuming responsibility for other people's feelings and happiness early in life, I grew up faster than I should have and became a caretaker and burden-bearer as an adult. I thought it was a good thing for me to be mature and responsible for my young age, but I wasn't a child long enough to know how to come as a child to the Father later in life. I had to find the lost little girl inside me in order for the adult me to get healed and transformed into the original, true identity my Father had for me as his child. Once I reclaimed that identity, I experienced a much greater range of emotions. Today I feel excitement and joy more deeply. I share my feelings toward others more freely, and I am more aware of pain and sadness and grief.

Henri Nouwen shares about his own brokenness:

> My own pain in life has taught me that the first step to healing is not a step away from the pain, but a step toward it. … We have to dare to overcome our fear and become familiar with it. Yes, we have to find the courage to embrace our own brokenness, to make our most feared enemy into a friend, and to claim it as an intimate companion. I am convinced that healing is often so difficult because we don't want to know the pain. Although this is true of all pain, it is especially true of the pain that comes from a broken heart. The anguish and agony that result from rejection, separation, neglect, abuse, and emotional manipulation serve only to paralyze us when we can't face them and keep running away from them. …
>
> My own experience with anguish has been that facing it and living it through is the way to healing. … Embracing it and bringing it into the light of the One who calls us the Beloved can make our brokenness shine like a diamond.[22]

The healing process is hard work. It is a roller coaster. There are days of giving up and days of reengaging. There are days when you can see so clearly—"I'm getting it!"—followed by days of denial. There are tears, anger, sadness, numbness, and wrestling with God. There is confusion—lots of confusion.

The Enemy will war against your heart; for he is fully aware that your heart, alive to God and alive to love, will destroy his hold on you. He won't be able to hook you in the same way ever again. Jesus said of Satan, "He has nothing in me" (John 14:30 NASB). The Enemy found nothing in Jesus to hook him with—no shame or blame or bitterness or resentment or doubt or rejection or fear. That is where the healing journey is taking you, so that you too can be free.

More Good News about Our Hearts

A few years ago, the Lord showed me (Denise) a picture of my heart, and there were major cracks in it. In the vision, Jesus was standing next to my heart in white masonry clothes, and he was holding a palette of mortar in one hand and a trowel in the other. He was taking the mortar and repairing all the major cracks in my heart and smoothing them over.

Then he showed me some pieces of my heart that lay shattered on the floor, too badly damaged to be repaired. I needed brand new parts. The Lord applied large portions of mortar to these areas and created a whole new heart.

I said, "Lord, that is great, but cement becomes hardened, and I don't want a hard heart!"

He didn't say anything, but took out his Bic lighter, flicked it, and set my heart on fire. The fire didn't mean I was "well done" (pun intended) with my healing, but that the fire of God's love for me, right there *with* me, would continue to warm, comfort, illuminate, and purify my heart on the journey of healing.

Now stop and ask, "Jesus, would you do the same thing for me? Jesus, would you heal my broken heart? Would you bind up all the broken places within me? Would you remove all the shame, all the guilt, all the fear, and all the performing? Would you exchange my heart for yours and make me fully alive again—or even alive for the first time?"

John Eldredge, in his book *Wild at Heart*, encourages us with the hope of Jesus coming to heal our hearts:

When the Bible tells us that Christ came to "redeem mankind" it offers a whole lot more than forgiveness. ... The core of Christ's mission is foretold in Isaiah 61:

The Spirit of the Sovereign Lord is on me,
because the Lord has anointed me
to preach good news to the poor.
He has sent me to bind up the brokenhearted,

to proclaim freedom for the captives
and release from darkness for the prisoners. (v. 1)

The Messiah will come, he says, to bind up and heal, to release and set free. What? *Your heart.* Christ comes to restore and release you, your soul, the true you. This is *the* central passage in the entire Bible about Jesus, the one he chooses to quote about himself when he steps into the spotlight in Luke 4 and announces his arrival. So take him at his word—and ask him in to heal all the broken places within you and unite them into one whole and healed heart. Ask him to release you from all bondage and captivity, as he promised to do.… But you can't do this at a distance; you can't ask Christ to come into your wound while you remain far from it. You have to go there with him.[23]

Restoring the Years

I (Denise) had a personal revelation about the Scripture in which God says, "I will restore to you the years that the swarming locust has eaten" (Joel 2:25 NKJV). The verse goes on to include "the crawling locust, the consuming locust, and the chewing locust." (It makes me want to stop and call my exterminator.) That's a lot of locust eating up a lot of years! Many of our clients identify with the statements, "I have wasted a lot of time and energy, some of my best years," and, "I have messed up so badly, I've missed God's best for me."

When a client is forty or fifty or seventy years old, it may seem impossible to get each calendar year back. But I believe God sees it from a different perspective. When God restores our true self, our God-created self, and redeems all the parts of us that we denied or even hated; when we can be free, innocent, vulnerable, and trusting as a child; when we can run into the throne of grace and climb up onto Papa God's lap—*then* all the years the locusts have eaten will indeed be restored. It is not the calendar years that are given back to us; rather, it is God going back in our lives and reclaiming every part of us that was broken, bruised, abandoned, and neglected. Our hearts are no longer divided or fragmented, but are in perfect union with his. Every part of us can now begin to love what he loves.

Who Is Driving Your Car?

When Trudy's dad got mad, he would yell and hit the wall or the dog. Sometimes he also beat her brother. When Trudy got in trouble, her dad would give her a long lecture, spank her, and then give her another long lecture. (We're talking *long* here—like an hour).

Because of how her dad had modeled the role of father when she was a girl, Trudy avoided time with God as an adult. She explained, "If I know God's in the room with me, I don't want to sit down with him. I'm like a nervous, pacing teenager full of anxiety because I know God is going to give me a lecture, just like Dad. I'm just afraid of what he is going to say. I am scared because maybe I've screwed up. I don't know how, but I always screw up. I just never know what I did. But, like my dad, God will make sure I find out."

The adult Trudy's emotions and scared reactions are really those expressed by the younger child within. We like to ask the counselee this question:

"How old is the child who is driving your emotional car, and is she old enough to have a license?"

Patricia remembers her father coming home from the war when she was four years old. She climbed up onto his lap and couldn't love on him enough. She was so happy he was home. Then something traumatic happened: her daddy took her arms off from around his neck and put her down on the floor away from him. Little Patti walked away with tears running down her face, and no one noticed.

Let us stop here as we interrupt Patti's story to ask you a question we posed previously. What was the Father *feeling* when that happened to Patti? Devastation? Pain? Anger? Sorrow? All the above?

I know that I felt my heart sink. Did God's too?

Without Patti realizing it, her heart put up a wall to protect herself from ever being hurt again—a wall that now hinders her intimacy with her new husband as well as with God.

So we ask the question, "How old is the child who is driving the adult Patricia's emotional car, and is she old enough to have a license?"

After sharing the above memory, Patricia shared her deepest heart cry, "I think if I sum it all up, what I want to feel the most is cherished. Because when you are cherished, you are loved, valued, and protected. That is what I want for myself and for that little four-year-old girl—that little Patti who lives inside of me."

We can look Patti straight in her eyes and tell her that this is what Father God wants for her too. He came to heal her broken heart.

Bob grew up in a very legalistic home. In church, if he even moved, his dad hit him on the head. Early on, Bob learned to conform, to be perfect, to never show anger, to be good, quiet, and nice. He was known as a calm person, he told us, and on his tombstone would be the inscription, "He was just a nice guy."

That's it. Not even his name.

Bob said, "My dad broke my spirit. I stopped being who I really was, and I learned to be who he wanted. That way I could look good and keep the peace."

But the Father showed Bob who he really was in the spirit realm: a *warrior*. The true self that the Father knit together in this baby boy had a heart like David, full of fierce passion and desire. To counter that, the Enemy sowed in Bob's soul seeds of compliance, passivity, resignation, fear of failure, shame, and the sense that he would never be good enough. Bob's destiny was to live fully alive in his warrior identity, but instead he learned to deaden his feelings so he could survive.

How old is the child who is driving the adult Bob's emotional car, and is he old enough to have a license?

Sandy grew up in an alcoholic home where both of her parents were addicted. She describes herself as just a stray on the street—orphaned.

She recalls that she was treated like a grown up and left in charge of her parents from the time she was a small child. When she was in kindergarten, she locked up the house at night because her mom and dad were passed out, drunk.

Today, Sandy believes God sees her, but he doesn't care about her. All she wants in her life is "someone to take care of me."

How old is the child who is driving the adult Sandy's emotional car, and is she old enough to have a license?

Recovering Your True, Childlike Self

We often ask our clients to write a letter to the child within, sharing what they believe this child needed to hear in the past and needs to hear from them now.

You as the adult self can play an important role in bringing love and security to these younger true parts of yourself. In a way, you can re-parent yourself by being good to yourself and believing in yourself and extending grace to yourself, just like the Father does.

"I'm supposed to write a letter to my child within? That sounds a little strange and uncomfortable, me writing to myself."

Stop and consider: when was the last time you talked to yourself? When you forgot to call your mom on her birthday? When you yelled at your kids for a problem that was your own issue? When you looked in the mirror and didn't like how you looked? When you asked God for help in making a decision and he didn't acknowledge you with an answer?

When such things happen, your inner self-talk (we call it your "shaming committee") might sound something like this:

"What an idiot I am!"
"I can't believe I am going to be late."
"What a klutz."
"I am so stupid."
"I am a bad mother."

"I can't stand my haircut."

"I am butt ugly."

"God is there for others, but not me."

"Maybe I need to read my Bible more and pray more and serve more."

Like the church sign down the road suggests, "Get right or get left." Or our personal beat-yourself-up guilt-trip favorite: "If God seems far away, guess who moved!" Loser!

The point is, you have conversations in your head all the time. Once you realize this, maybe writing a letter to your vulnerable inner child won't seem so hard or weird. There is one condition, though: *what you write has to agree with what God would say about you.*

Here are letters our counselees have shared, beginning with this one written to a little lost girl.

Little me,

Would you like to come home? Would you like a home that you so longed for but didn't have? I want to create a different place for you where you no longer wander off and get lost in the shadow of others. I need you to be complete. I want to hear about all your adventures and see what you're like. I know I've missed out on a lot by not acknowledging you. People tell me all the time that I don't know how to have fun—that I am too serious. I lost that inner spark a long time ago and it was you! So, I need you. Isn't that nice to hear after all these years? Someone actually needs YOU in order to be fulfilled and whole.

Love you,
Me

A letter to an eight-year-old boy who was sexually abused by a teen neighbor girl:

Dear little boy,

I am writing you this letter because I want to connect with you and make you a part of my life again. I am so sorry for the hatred and disgust I have always felt towards you. I have totally locked you away and have never wanted to see you again. I am so sorry I have rejected you. For so many years I blamed you for what happened. I felt like you should have said "No" or spoke up or done something. I realize now it never was your fault and you were the victim. I did not realize how much I hated you and didn't want anything to do with you until recently.

I am so sorry for rejecting you for so many years. I want to get to know you better and heal my relationship with you. I am just realizing who you really were deep down in your heart and I am so sorry you never were able to be who you really were. I hope you will forgive me and together we can allow the Father to heal us and we can both learn together what really is deep down in our heart and what the Father created us to be.

I wish I could have been there to hold you and let you cry and release the pain you felt inside. I want you to know you are special and you do have what it takes. Your mother and father should have noticed you. It was not your fault. It was about their stuff and was not about something wrong or defective in you.

I am sorry I never loved you before but I do love you now, and I invite you to be my friend just because I think you're special, not because of what you do or the abilities you have. Please feel free to relax and just be you!

A letter to an unwanted and abused little boy:

Hi little boy— just want to connect with you. I know I never have until this point. I am just now seeing that no one really loved you and you really didn't belong. You were not special in anyone's eyes. It never really mattered what happened on a daily basis. Your voice and opinion never mattered. I remember your high school graduation and that no one came to support you. As for your home, it was not a safe environment. You were constantly walking in fear due to the beatings, threats, and violence.

Today for the first time in a long time, I am understanding how you felt—that you never were validated—you never were loved. That must have been so painful as a little boy—even over all these past years you still wanted to hide—just like you did back then. I remember when your dad came home and it was best to not be seen or heard! Oh … and I almost forgot how you must have felt at the dinner table—the fear of receiving your next beating—and how you must have felt going to your bedroom and crying out saying, "Why me? How come I can't have a normal family?"

Little boy, I just want you to know that today I want to connect with you and say it was none of your fault—you were just trying to survive. You are worthy of love and you belong to an incredible father—Father God. He was there with you when you were going through those tough times and He wept with you and He allowed you to use those defense mechanisms so you could make it through the bad stuff. But now, things are going to be different—now you and me are going to trust Him.

I love that little boy—YOU—unconditionally. I want you to feel free to share any memories from the past and I will be there to listen and understand.

We're gonna make it!

A follow-up letter from Caroline regarding her identity:

Dear Jerry and Denise,

After my last session, I have a new inner strength to acknowledge and own my thoughts and feelings. I can even acknowledge my existence without any guilt or condemnation. I also seem to be able to embrace my uniqueness and don't have to be so hard on myself. I have never been able to discern other people's stuff from my own, and not take it on as my fault or my problem. Being able to release other people's problems to God and not pick them up has reduced my anger and my stress significantly.

It seems that owning my right to exist is changing many relationship dynamics. I am calling forth in prayer the very personality that God made me to be. I am learning to discover my own likes, dislikes, thoughts and desires. With all of these revelations comes a fresh accountability for my own bad choices, as well as no longer feeling responsible for the bad choices of others. I am beginning to be free to develop my uniqueness without feeling the responsibility to earn the right to exist by fixing everyone's problems. This is all new and quite a daily struggle. Your prayer and counsel helped me begin to do what I knew in my head to do, but could not successfully follow through. This set up a guilt/condemnation cycle for me that until now I was never able to break. I only wish I could have come to you as a young person instead of waiting until I am in my sixties.

Gratefully,
Caroline

PRAYER

Lord Jesus, I want to live from a place of trust—trusting in you and your goodness and trusting others who you say are trustworthy. I also want to be able to trust my own heart that you have renewed by my faith in you.

Lord, help me to see if trust was broken in my early development. If so, I invite you to bring healing to that broken part of me. Jesus, if my identity as your child has been impaired from this early wounding, heal and restore me and help me to rest in who you've made me to be. I ask that you would help me to love the little child inside me the way you do. I need you, and I need every part of me that you created. Only you can bring about this healing and restoration in me. I choose to trust you in this—with me. In your name I pray, amen.

QUESTIONS FOR REFLECTION

1. Begin this time by reading the prayer above and making it your own.

2. Two early building blocks in a child's development are presented in this chapter: trust and identity. If trust is established, we are able to hold our hearts open to love. With identity, we establish a core sense that "I am me and I am okay." What deficits can you identify in these areas for yourself? Going back through the beginning of the chapter, what struggles do you experience that would suggest a breach in either the trust or identity stages of development?

3. What examples can you identify in your adult life in which your emotions or reactions are really those of a younger child within? *How old is this child who is driving the adult's emotional car, and is he or she old enough to have a license?*

4. INNER CHILD PICTURE EXERCISE

   • Find a picture of yourself at the earliest age you remember (before age six is best).

   • Close your eyes and picture the house you lived in when you were this age. Write down a brief description.

   • Now picture yourself opening up the front door to this house. What do you see? Describe what the front room looked like—then the rest of the rooms.

   • Try to picture your mother. Where is she? What is she doing?

   • And your father. Where is he? What is he doing?

   • Where are your siblings (if applicable)? What are they doing?

   • Now picture your room. What did it look like?

   • Picture yourself sitting on your bed in your room. What are you wearing? What are you doing? How are you feeling?

   • Now look at the photograph intently for about one minute. What do you see? How do you feel about yourself at this age? Write down the first feelings or thoughts that come to mind as you look at your picture. How do you feel about the child in the picture? What is the child like?

- Look again at the picture or visualize yourself sitting on your bed. Complete the following statements:
  - When I see me in the picture, I want to _____.
  - When I look at myself as a child in the picture, I want to _____.
  - Is this child happy? Why or why not?
  - Do you like this child? Why or why not?
  - How do you feel about your child within (which is still a part inside of you) as you look at the picture?
  - How do you think the Father *feels* about this child?
- Visualize yourself in the picture or on your bed and write your inner child a short letter, letting this child know whatever first comes to mind. Now place your pen in your OPPOSITE hand and write (print) a note back from the little child to the grownup you. Write the first thoughts that come to mind.

CHAPTER SEVEN

SHIELDS UP: THE WAYS WE PROTECT OURSELVES

The trouble with steeling yourself against the harshness of reality is that the same steel that secures your life against being destroyed secures your life also against being opened up and transformed.
—Frederick Buechner

The Origin and Power of Defense Mechanisms

Children come into this world with physical *and* emotional needs. Although the physical needs may often be met, many of the emotional needs are not. These emotional needs are not optional but essential in the healthy development of children as they progress and mature.

What happens when these needs are not met? How does a child deal with the pain from feeling rejected, neglected, or emotionally abandoned? These feelings in a child originate from parents who are well-meaning but unavailable emotionally as well as from parents and others who are overtly abusive. When children do not receive the necessary nurture and affection that God designed them to receive, they develop difficulties in trusting others, including God, later in life. In more and more families, children are expected to meet the needs of the parents while their own needs go unmet. And since children do not know what to do with the tremendous emotional pain of unmet needs, they learn to survive by developing defense mechanisms to protect themselves.

Unfortunately, we do not outgrow the defense mechanisms that we needed as children. Instead, we carry them into adulthood and into our relationships. These defenses keep the unreleased pain of the past stuffed down inside us. What helped us to survive as children—what was even provided by God for a helpless child—will no longer work in our favor as adults.

Where do self-protective mechanisms come from, and how do they originate in us? From the broadest perspective, our reliance on self-protection originated when Eve listened to the serpent in the garden and she and her willing husband ate from the tree of the knowledge of good and evil (Genesis 3:6). In so doing, they chose to trust in their own reasoning instead of God. Their first action following this deception was to *protect themselves,* sewing fig leaves together to cover their nakedness and shame (Genesis 3:7).

In our first psychology class, we learned about defense mechanisms. At the time, we saw their relevance from a strictly psychological perspective. But soon in our counseling ministry, we began to see defense mechanisms from a totally different perspective—a spiritual one. In order to help people experience healing from their emotional wounds, we began to address the "shields" that guarded their hearts not only from being hurt, but also from being fully engaged and alive.

They had thought it necessary to trust in their own means of protection rather than trusting in God's love, truth, and power to protect them. By exchanging their trust in self for trust in God, they positioned themselves for breakthrough into deeper heart healing.

Examples of Defense Mechanisms

The following defense mechanisms are the ones most commonly identified by our clients. As you read each one, ask yourself whether it applies to you. It's common to identify several.

Denial: a common defense mechanism whereby we consciously or subconsciously refuse to accept the reality of an event or situation.

Denial is often considered a blind spot: it is difficult to see unless others point it out to us. For example, a husband who has obvious problems in his marriage says, "I have a good marriage. Everything is fine." He denies reality in order to avoid dealing with the truth.

Denial is also characteristic in addictions:

"I only drink beer, so I can't be an alcoholic."

"I had a couple of one night stands, but it wasn't adultery."

"No one's perfect. Who hasn't looked at pornography?"

Minimization: closely related to denial, minimization decreases the importance or significance of something.

Let's say that you had a very painful childhood. Yet when confronted with that fact, you say, "It wasn't that bad. Many people had it worse than I did." Maybe you add, "My parents did the best they could. They had a rough childhood too." That may be true, but if it stops you from owning the full truth of what happened to you growing up, you will never get to a deeper level of healing. If you convince yourself that what occurred to you didn't matter or was insignificant or unavoidable, then there isn't anything to invite God to heal.

Remember, our viewpoints and resulting conclusions must agree with what God says about the situation. Did God say to you, "I'm sorry, but your parents had no option when raising you other than to pass on the same bad parenting they received to you?" Of course not. We believe that the heart of God is to heal each generation that invites him to do so. We do not believe that the subsequent generations are destined to repeat and relive the wounding from the past.

Taking your parents off the hook *at the end* of the healing process, *after* working through the pain, loss, grief, and forgiveness, is different from giving them a pass at the front end of the process as an excuse for their sinful behavior. Choosing to release them at the end is the last stage of grieving, and this is acceptance, not minimization.

Emotional insulation: withdrawing in order to avoid rejection.

With this mechanism, we either physically withdraw from situations such as church, social gatherings, or relationships; or we close off our hearts and don't feel much because we have learned to stuff down our emotions.

Dissociation: disconnecting or escaping from what is happening in our world around us at the moment.

There are different degrees of dissociation. The most minimal is when we "zone out" for a few moments or a short time. Some victims of violence or abuse have learned to separate themselves during the event, such that they can actually watch the abuse from outside their bodies and avoid the feelings of fear, terror, pain, and shame. In dissociative identity disorder, victims of trauma fragment themselves and form different personalities. In some abusive situations, this may be the only means for the child to survive the abuse.

Compartmentalizing: taking an act or circumstance that is disturbing, distressful, or painful and mentally placing it on the shelf or filing it away so that it does not affect other parts of our lives.

For example, a married couple is ready to sign the divorce papers. They have no emotional or spiritual intimacy. Yet they have good sexual relations. They have learned to compartmentalize the other issues of their marriage from their sexual needs.

Another example: a person who experienced severe childhood abuse has mentally placed that abuse in its own box or compartment. Thus, the painful past does not overtly touch other parts of that person's life or relationships.

When a secret exists in the marriage relationship, such as pornography or adultery, compartmentalizing allows the guilty person to function almost as if the infidelity isn't real. The offended spouse may ask, "How could you not think of me or the family?" One answers: compartmentalizing.

God desires that we live from a place of unity within. Just as unity among brothers and sisters in Christ commands the blessing of God (Psalm 133), we believe that when we live from a place of unity within instead of with fragmented hearts, we invite the fullness of God's blessing and favor. God created us to be integrated, not fragmented.

Regression: *reverting mentally to a younger, less mature way of handling stresses and feelings.*

A young woman has a confrontation with her roommate, stomps out of the room, locks herself in her bedroom, and won't come out. That's regression in operation.

Driving erratically, refusing to get out of bed, throwing the phone across the room, or pouting are other examples of childish responses to bad feelings.

Fantasy or Pretending: *avoiding reality by creating images or dreams in our imagination.*

We may pretend that something not real is true, or that we are doing something beyond our ability. A man may imagine that he is next in line for a partnership at work or that he was such a good high school quarterback that he could have played professional football. He gets lost in these thoughts on a regular basis. This is more than simply daydreaming or imagining good things for the future. It is a way to escape the present.

Displacement: *taking out our frustrations on others.*

We feel pain or stress over a past or current situation or event and then take out our frustration or anger on a family member or friend. Displacement is often referred to as the "mad at the boss but kick the dog" syndrome.

Projection: *blaming others for things that are not their fault.*

We feel bad about something we said or did, but instead of taking responsibility for our action and feeling healthy shame, we blame it on someone or something else.

Self-projection: *a form of projection in which we don't blame others but instead blame ourselves.*

"It's my fault." "I can't do anything right." "I deserve it." Such self-blame hinders true, God-initiated, heartfelt repentance.

Both other- and self-projection are often the result of destructive shame, when we do not feel good about who we are.

Defensive anger: a mechanism closely related to displacement and projection in which we use anger as a defensive shield.

While some resources don't define anger as a defense mechanism, we believe that in certain situations it indeed serves as such. Anger is a crucial emotion, and although we can sin in the way we express it, anger in itself is not sinful (Ephesians 4:26). Anger can be a pointer to another emotion that needs to be addressed, such as pain, fear, disappointment, loss, betrayal, or injustice.

However, when we disregard the underlying emotions and simply allow anger to manifest, then it can begin to take on a life of its own. It becomes a source of defense and power that blocks the deeper issues and the hurts that need to be expressed. When anger reaches this level, it is a strong defense mechanism that must be addressed.

Self-sufficiency or Self-reliance: avoiding our feelings by becoming strong in our own ability.

Self-sufficiency manifests in statements such as, "I'm a survivor." "I can make it." "I can't count on anyone else, but I can always count on me." We fit the description of a self-contained unit. We do not allow ourselves to *need*, and we find it hard to receive help from others. We may pride ourselves in our own independence. We cannot easily acknowledge our weakness or dependency on God or others, and we frequently attempt to control situations. But although we may look strong on the outside, the driver inside us is fear.

Rationalization: seeking to defend ourselves by justifying or excusing our actions.

One who is rationalizing might say, "If you only knew my situation, you would understand why I am the way I am." Or, "No one in my family ever says 'I love you'—that's just the way we are." Or, "I'm sorry I yelled at you, but you hurt me by not talking to me last night just because I was late for dinner."

Whenever we add the word *but* or want to follow an apology with an explanation for our behavior, we need to stop and check if we are being defensive and rationalizing.

Intellectualization: seeking a logical explanation for a problem or issue in order to avoid feelings.

For instance, a woman shares with her coworker that she feels depressed and hopeless about her future. The coworker responds, "Why would you be depressed? Just think of all the many things you should be thankful for."

Or a wife comes home from work feeling frustrated over a meeting that went poorly, and her husband goes into fix-it mode by addressing the facts of the problem while ignoring his wife's need to be listened to, understood, and validated.

These and other mechanisms of defense have one thing in common: they place us, rather than God, in control of our lives. As a result, our relationship with him suffers and we are left unhealed.

Inner Vows: A Clenched Fist in Our Heart

Another powerful form of self-protection is an *inner vow*. This is a decision we make in our heart or spirit, often at a young age, that affects and even directs our life in subsequent years.

Inner vows usually come from strong feelings rather than rational thinking and decision-making. An inner vow is like a clenched fist in our heart: we make a strong decision about someone or something in order to protect ourselves from hurt or pain.

Scripture contains ample examples of vows made before God, such as wedding vows. But we are not to make vows that are not consistent with the heart and will of God. Vows made from a self-protective motive can have a significant negative impact on our lives, especially vows made when we were young and most vulnerable. Such vows may have been spoken verbally, but often they were simply made internally as a means of avoiding pain. If we made such vows when we were young, we may not even remember doing so. The proof, however, is when we can look at the course of our adult life, especially our relationships, and see our life going in the direction of an inner vow.

An inner vow is often preceded by the words "I will never" or "I will always." Here are some examples:[24]

"I Will Never" Vows

I will never let anyone love me. I will never be loved just for me. I will never be weak. I will never be wanted. I will never trust anyone. I will never allow myself to need anyone or anything. I will never let anyone take anything away from me. I will never allow anyone to touch me. I will never share what is mine. I will never allow anyone to give me money. I will never be able to understand or "get it." I will never go out at night. I will never let you see who I really am. I will never let anyone know I hurt (physically or emotionally). I will never tell a woman (or a man) anything. I will never let a man (or a woman) control me. I will never be responsible for the actions of others. I will never receive a compliment. I will never participate fully in life. I will never allow a woman (or a man) into my heart. I will never be anything worthwhile. I will never grow up and be mature. I will never be angry. I will never know who I am. I will never belong. I will never be pleasing. I will never cry. I will never have children. I will never know what to do with my life.

"I Will Always" Vows

I will always remain aloof. I will always be separate. I will always be invisible and compliant. I will always be afraid. I will always be rejected. I will always be in control. I will always be single. I will always be logical. I will always be strong. I will always be damaged goods. I will always be used or abused. I will always be in pain. I will always be poor. I will always be on the outside looking in.

"I Will Never Be Angry": A Personal Example

When I (Jerry) was young, I made a number of decisions in my heart that impacted my adult life. The one that stands out the most is the inner vow, "I will never be angry."

My father easily became irritated and impatient, and his anger and rage could come out suddenly and when least expected. As a child, I hated his anger because of how anxious it made me feel and how it affected the rest of the family, especially my mother. I don't remember ever making a vow not to be angry, but as I became older, and especially when I married Denise, I never did anger. It wasn't that things didn't make me frustrated, irritated, or upset. I just never let others know that I was angry, especially the person who was the object of my anger. Rather, I stuffed my anger, which was not only unhealthy for me but also made the stuffed part of my heart unavailable to God, Denise, and others.

Since the only picture of anger I had growing up led me to believe it was hurtful, shameful, and wrong, I wanted nothing to do with it. So I shut down all feelings of anger. Had you asked me whether I had ever decided, "I will never be angry," I would have quickly answered no. But upon looking closely at my life and relationships, I realized that the way I related with others proved that I had indeed made such a vow.

If the words *always* or *never* are too strong for you because the statement isn't true for you all the time, then step back and examine it from a broader perspective. For instance, you may not feel that you *always* have to be in control of everything; yet most of the time, that is how you live or feel most comfortable. If so, then look for a possible inner vow that started early in your life.

The more control we need in our adult life, the more out-of-control or chaotic our childhood has usually been. Becoming aware of the inner vows you have made will help you connect with the pain and grief of the child inside you, who was trying to cope with difficult surroundings growing up.

"Good" Vows Are Still Bad Vows

Sometimes we make vows that would be considered positive, yet in reality they hinder us. For instance, someone who grew up in a violent or abusive home may have made the vow, "I will never be violent or abusive." That seems like a good thing to decide. However, when we make clenched-fist-in-my-heart decisions—even ones that produce good behavior—we are still depending on our own ability or righteousness to do what's good and avoid what's bad. We are not trusting in God and depending on his ability, his strength, to help us maintain good, godly behavior.

This doesn't mean that, as adults, we should perpetuate the destructive behavior we observed as children. It does mean, however, that we must come to a place of realizing that we can do nothing apart from the grace of God.

Fortified Walls Yield Hearts of Stone

Defense mechanisms and inner vows place our trust in our own power rather than in God to be our defense, our protection, and our strength. These self-built walls of protection become fortified in us over the years and result in our hearts growing hardened or detached from God. The Lord is jealous for us and our affections (Exodus 20:5) and asks us to love him with *all* of our heart (Luke 10:27). But we cannot fully give to him and receive from him until we allow him to take down our walls.

These walls of defense around our hearts correlate with the fortified cities in the Old Testament. Moses warned the Israelites that disobedience to God would result in the Lord's bringing a nation against them that would "lay siege to all the cities until *the high fortified walls in which you trust fall down*" (Deuteronomy 28:49, 52, italics added). Jeremiah reiterated this prophetic message of warning, stating that "[a distant nation] will destroy *the fortified cities in which you trust*" (Jeremiah 5:17, italics added).

The various mechanisms we use as adults to protect ourselves are a form of demonic deception. Misled to believe that we can and must take up our own defense, we lean on our own understanding rather than trusting in the Lord (Proverbs 3:5).

But if we have placed our trust in Jesus Christ, then he in turn has done what Ezekiel 36:26 promises: "I will give you a new heart and put a new spirit in you; I will remove from you your heart of stone and give you a heart of flesh." Jesus invites us to yield our hearts to him fully and thus *experience* what has already occurred.

Inviting Godly Weakness

Positive fruit results from revealing and dealing with our defenses; yet many struggle with choosing this path. Why? Because facing and feeling the unresolved pain of the past requires that we become weak and vulnerable, something we may have worked much of our adult lives to avoid. Many equate giving up their self-defense mechanisms to being totally defenseless. These people have learned to survive on their own power all their lives. When there was no one else to trust, when everyone else let them down, they knew they could always count on themselves. They toughened up and didn't need anyone. Logically, then, they might ask, "Why would I ever want to pray down my defenses and open up my heart to feel? Why would I want to go back there and feel that way again? What good did it do for me then, and how in the world could it do me any good now?"

Nevertheless, the only effective way we know to find deep healing for the heart is to embrace godly weakness. Brokenness is where the rubber truly meets the road when it comes to trusting our Savior, Jesus, who came to heal the brokenhearted and set the captives free (Luke 4:18). We must acknowledge that our hearts are broken and, to varying degrees, held in captivity.

The apostle Paul came to this awareness as he cried out multiple times for Christ to intervene in his struggle. Jesus's response, "My grace is sufficient for you, for my power is made perfect in weakness" (2 Corinthians 12:9), changed something in Paul. He didn't run or hide from his weakness. Rather, he wrote, "I will boast all the more gladly about my weaknesses, so that Christ's power may rest on me" (2 Corinthians 12:9).

Once you become willing to embrace godly weakness in place of defense mechanisms and inner vows, you are ready to take your shields down. The first step is to acknowledge all of your defenses to God. Then share with him what you are willing to change. Finally, ask for and receive his forgiveness. For example, if you realize that you made a vow, "I will never allow anyone to know that I hurt," simply pray aloud something like this:

"Lord, I renounce the vow that I will never allow anyone to know that I hurt. By your grace, I am willing to begin to let others to whom you direct me know when I am hurting."

Then continue with the next vow:

"Lord, I renounce the vow that I will always be strong. By your grace, I am willing to be weak so that you can be strong in me."

Next, the defense mechanisms:

"Lord, I acknowledge that I have used *minimization* as a means to protect myself from feeling pain. If you say something is a big deal, then I want it to be a big deal to me.

"I also acknowledge that I have used *emotional insulation* to avoid rejection by others. I want to learn how to engage with others and not hide from relationships."

When you are finished with your acknowledgements, simply conclude in prayer:

"Thank you for forgiving me, Lord. I receive your forgiveness, and I forgive myself."

By acknowledging to God the ways we have protected ourselves, we break the power of the Enemy's deception and set in motion the transfer of trust from ourselves to God. Doing so often serves as a dramatic first step in the healing process.

The Grace to Change

Giving up our own strength and embracing weakness in order to more fully experience the kingdom of God isn't very appealing, especially in our western culture. It may sound like foolishness to many. But "God chose the foolish things of the world to shame the wise; God chose the weak things of the world to shame the strong" (1 Corinthians 1:27).

Note that becoming weak, vulnerable, and defenseless does not mean that we become a doormat for others. What it does mean is that we seek God's discernment on how to handle a given situation rather than responding out of our previous methods of defense.

For example, if someone you encounter is emotionally unsafe, God might direct you to communicate a godly boundary in that situation.

Or perhaps someone is doing or saying something hurtful to you. As you seek God's heart on the matter, he may direct you to confront that person in love in an effort to preserve or restore the relationship through honesty—hard to do if your typical defense is to withdraw. On the other hand, if your normal defense is aggression, then God may lead you in a different, equally difficult direction: to say nothing at first, but rather, to wait and ask God if, when, and how you should respond.

In situations such as these, you will learn to relinquish your control to God, seek to hear from him, and then respond accordingly.

Will the protective mechanisms you have used all your life simply go away? No. But in time, you will begin to see changes taking place in your heart and actions. If you are serious with God about wanting to change, he will show you when you are relying on one of your past defenses instead of him. Often the Holy Spirit will nudge you when you are on the verge of responding in an old, self-protective way. Then the choice is before you. However, understand that the Father has much grace for you as you seek to walk out this new way of living. He doesn't expect perfection; he only asks for a willing heart and the humility to admit to him and those around you when you have blown it and need to start afresh.

The following illustration spoke to the two of us on our personal healing paths, and we use it with our clients. It dramatizes how the Father heals and frees the wounded parts of our heart as we "expose them to the light."

When I was a kid, we had a pile of discarded lumber sitting next to the house which we would play in. During the early summer, as we cleaned up the yard, I had to pick up a board which had been left lying on the lawn. When I did so, I exposed a patch of dirt that had been cut off from the sun, on which no grass could grow.

Exposed to the light, all of the earwigs, sow bugs, and spiders went scurrying. It was truly ugly under that board! Only a few yellowish strands of grass searched desperately for the edge of the board and the sunlight.

I was tempted to leave the board where it had been because it looked better than that bare spot on the lawn. But the board got tossed, and the ugly bare spot remained exposed to the light.

As summer progressed, though, and the lawn got watered, mowed and lit by the sun, the spot filled in with grass. By the end of the summer, no one would have known that the ugly spot had ever been there.[25]

It can be the same way in our healing journey. When we expose what lies hidden within us, the light of the truth can shine on those places. The process will probably be painful and we will be tempted to hide the ugly stuff again. However, if we invite the Holy Spirit to be here with us on this heart-healing path, then the light will do its work. And in due season, the hidden area will be healed.

In her book *In the Voice of a Child*, Judy Emerson shares what she learned about self-protective mechanisms during her healing journey from sexual abuse:

> If I ask a medical doctor to heal a wound in my physical body, he will insist that I remove the four layers of clothing covering it up. He has to examine the hurt first. For a therapist to help me heal a spiritual and emotional wound, he will ask me to remove the rationalizations and defense mechanisms disguising it. We have to examine the hurt. We have to assess the extent of the damage so the cure will be complete.…
>
> Saying the words about what happened back then draws us out of denial and allows us to admit our need. And it breaks the chains that secrecy creates.… Because when we expose it to the light of Christ, we aren't bound by it anymore.[26]

The Lord seeks broken and contrite hearts (Psalm 51:17) that believe he is good and trustworthy and has our best interests in mind. He desires us to have a greater level of intimacy with him and a greater ability for us to give and receive love—including love for ourselves. He wants to pour out his "kindness which leads us to (change) repentance" (Romans 2:4) and break away anything that would block such a gift. Will you choose him over your fear? Will you begin to bring down your shields? Are you willing to trust him?

PRAYER

Father, I need your help. I know that I have developed ways to protect myself from pain, especially pain that started long ago. I need you to show me the ways in which I have done this. Although I am uneasy and even fearful of opening this door, I want to live from the place of "abundant life" that your Son came to give me.

As you expose the ways I have learned to protect myself, please give me the grace to reject my self-made shields and mechanisms. I invite you in to defend and protect me. I ask you to make me weak with a godly weakness so that I can live from your strength. Lord, I ask you to make me defenseless in my own ability so that you can truly be my defense. And I tell you that I am willing to feel what you would have me feel, no more and no less than you say is necessary. I am willing, by your grace, to be emotionally honest, transparent, and vulnerable before you and before others who you say are trustworthy. I pray all of this in the name of your Son, Jesus, amen.

QUESTIONS FOR REFLECTION

1. Review the section on "Examples of Defense Mechanisms." Which ones can you identify in yourself? (It may be helpful to ask someone close to you what they see in you, since you may not see some of the defenses in yourself).

2. Reflect on the following: All defense mechanisms have one thing in common: they place us, rather than God, in control of our lives. As a result, our relationship with him suffers and we are left unhealed. Is this a new revelation for you? Explain. Are you willing to place God in control of your life? Why or why not?

3. Which of the "I will never" and "I will always" inner vows can you identify in your life? In what ways might they have hardened your heart?

4. Are you willing at this point to embrace godly weakness—that is, to give up your own strength in exchange for God's? What feelings does the thought of doing so evoke in you? Sometimes resistance in this area provides clues to past wounds. If you experience such resistance, ask God to show you what the block is about.

5. When you are ready, find a quiet place and bring the sacrifice God desires: a broken and contrite heart. Offer him your self-protective shields, knowing that he plans to heal the inner pain that you have wanted to avoid facing.

6. Reread the closing prayer aloud and make it your own. Keep this truth up front: Jesus came to heal the brokenhearted and set the captives free—and that includes healing *your* heart and setting *you* free.

CHAPTER EIGHT

SHAME AND THE LIES WE BELIEVE

*I have never known who I really was because my whole life
I have been wearing a mask, performing for and trying to
please others. My mother even made me dress up with full
makeup and my hair done to go to the mailbox—because
"you never know if someone will see you."*
—*A teen during her recovery from anorexia*

Understanding Healthy Shame

Many people misunderstand shame. Let's get an accurate understanding
of shame in its two forms: healthy and toxic.

Shame often results from having done something that is embarrass-
ing, disgraceful, appalling, or discrediting. Maybe you made a mistake at
work that negatively impacted your department. Many people knew that
you caused the problem. It was just human error, but you feel ashamed
nonetheless. This type of shame in its appropriate form lets you know that
you have limitations and will make mistakes.

Or maybe you told a lie, or took a less-than-stellar shortcut on your
report, or vented your personal frustrations on your spouse. You knew it
was wrong, but you did it anyway. Such actions should also produce a feeling of shame. Healthy shame allows you to feel pain or sorrow when you
violate God-designed ways of loving yourself and others. Shame over sin—

or "missing the mark" of God's ways—is intended to bring about the good fruit of godly sorrow that leads to repentance (2 Corinthians 7:9–11).

Healthy shame is often used interchangeably with the term *true guilt*. Feeling this type of shame leads us to make things right with those affected by our actions. When possible, we can work to correct the results of what we've done. In the case of a relationship, we can seek reconciliation and restoration. Even if we cannot reverse the results of our action or lack of action, we can still take responsibility for it. Most importantly, we can acknowledge to God that we're truly sorry for what occurred. Asking for and receiving his forgiveness through Jesus Christ, and then forgiving ourselves, lets us move forward with new hope.

All of the above are reasons why God, through the Holy Spirit living in us, lets us experience and process healthy shame.

Toxic Shame

Ungodly *toxic shame* is much different from healthy shame. It is one of the most prevalent and harmful issues that we address in counseling. Toxic shame robs us of the life that the Father intends for us to experience. It interferes with living passionately as lovers of God and our fellow humans.

Toxic shame reveals itself in multiple ways. It commonly manifests as a hopeless, painful belief that a part of us is defective, bad, phony, inadequate, or a failure. We may experience a sense of worthlessness, of having little or no value. We feel isolated and alienated, different from and less than others. We judge ourselves and become an object of our own contempt.

Through self-shaming, we become our own tormentor, gaining ground for the Enemy. Little about us satisfies or pleases us; we can, however, always find plenty to criticize. Judging ourselves by ideal standards, we doom ourselves to repeatedly prove the obvious: that we can never "do it good enough."

Our self-judging blocks genuine conviction by the Holy Spirit, and thus, true repentance and change.

Besides causing us to feel defective or inadequate, toxic shame also convinces us that others can see through us, past our false front and directly into our defects. In response, we may physically withdraw from people, or we may emotionally hide by projecting a facade that protects our true self.

Toxic shame makes us afraid to share our inner self, because if we do, we may not be accepted for whom we really are. Instead, we often learn to project an image of what we think others want to see. Exposing our true self seems too naked, too vulnerable. The risk of rejection is too great, the fear too formidable. Thus, we learn a crucial rule for life: *Avoid shame at all costs.*

Faces of Toxic Shame

Ask yourself the following questions (and in addition, ask those closest to you how they would answer them about you):

- Do I become defensive with others?
- Am I critical of myself and others?
- Is my self-talk negative, condemning, and merciless?
- Am I a perfectionist?
- Am I performance-driven, a human doing versus a human being?
- Do I fear closeness and intimacy, craving it yet fleeing from it?
- Do I isolate physically—or emotionally, shutting down or stuffing my feelings?
- Am I controlling of others?
- Do I have difficulty identifying or expressing feelings?
- Am I a people-pleaser, longing for approval and recognition?
- Do I have difficulty trusting others, including God?
- Am I sensitive to criticism, even when it's constructive?
- Is it hard for me to admit I am wrong and say I am sorry?
- Do I need to be right in order to feel better about myself?

- Do I have difficulty making decisions?
- Do I find myself trying to prove I am okay by working harder or doing more?
- Do I struggle with addictive behaviors?

A "yes" answer to any of these questions points to a wound of shame.

The Controlling Side of Toxic Shame

Some of our clients do not relate to the symptoms of toxic shame that we've just identified. Yet these people struggle in significant ways in their relationships with God and with others. As they look deeper into the reasons behind their difficulties, toxic shame surfaces—but in a different form. We call it *controlling* or *aggressive shame*, but it is shame nonetheless.

This kind of shame allows no room for feelings of inferiority, inadequacy, or failure. Personal strength and self-will dominate. Feelings, good or bad, have little place. Such an individual may present as being demanding, rigid and inflexible, in control. They may appear to disregard the needs and opinions of others. Their objective is to succeed, to look good, to be right, and get it right. With this type of shame, open, honest, and vulnerable relationships are difficult to achieve. But unless you are in a close relationship with someone influenced by controlling shame, you would not know of the relational consequences it produces.

Great, unseen fear underlies such a person's external drivenness. It is not overt fear, such as a fear of heights or a fear of public speaking. Rather, it is a deep-seated, core fear, such as the fear of not being in control; the fear of not having what it takes to succeed; the fear of failure, which points to a core of insecurity. But this kind of person has learned to compensate for their deep issue of shame in a way that conceals it. What might be more evident is his or her need to assert control, resist control, or both.

While such individuals typically exhibit few feelings, the one emotion they do often display is anger, and others are well aware of it. Anger is an important emotion, and it generally points to other feelings such as loss, disappointment, hurt, and betrayal. But anger can also be used as a defense to deal with deeper levels of fear and insecurity.

Since such people are often successful in the ways that society views success, many often applaud them. But the motivation behind their success is shame: making sure that the deep-seated feelings of inadequacy are never seen by others—nor by them.

The truth emerges, however, when the measures of success get stripped away. Failing health, financial failure, marriage problems … losses of various kinds begin to accumulate. When the losses exceed the strength of a person's defense mechanisms, then the strong, external false self that conceals the shame-based identity begins at last to decay and fall away. Now real healing can commence. Unfortunately, by this time, considerable damage in important relationships has already occurred.

Toxic Shame Produces Pride

Toxic shame results in either of two forms of pride. It may be the pride that says, "I can do this. I can survive and overcome and be victorious and show you that I am someone." Or it is the pride that says, "I am so inadequate and so defective that I can never be healed and I'll never change." This latter kind of pride is often termed *the pride of the worm.* The person is saying, in essence, that he is too big of a problem—even for God.

Although it may sometimes be important to confront pride from a spiritual perspective, we find it more important and effective to deal with the underlying fear—since *fear is typically at the base of pride.* According to 1 John 4:18, "There is no fear in love. But perfect love drives out fear." A proud person—which is to say, a fearful person— needs love to fill the places in her where fear lives. We believe that God's ultimate goal is to bring his love to those deep places, and thus it is our goal as well.

The Internal War over Our Identity

As believers in Christ, we are defined by God as holy and righteous—as *saints*. This is how God sees us. Yet I (Jerry) have battled greatly over the years to see myself in the same way. Why? Why is it easy for some to accept their new identity in Christ while others like me find it so much more difficult?

Denise and I believe that much of the reason lies in whether, as a child, a person received the messages that were necessary to establish the foundation for accepting and embracing themselves and others.

In my case, missing pieces in my development as a child convinced me, deep in my heart, that "I am me and I am not okay" rather than "I am me and I am okay." This wasn't a matter I gave serious thought to before reaching my conclusion; children do not have that kind of cognitive ability. Until age five, children are really just bags of feelings. Their world revolves around what they feel and perceive. Their sense of worth and value comes through their hearts and spirits, not their minds. So as I continued to grow, I struggled with a shame-based identity—not feeling good enough—and it set me up for a great deal of fear and anxiety. I wanted not only to do well and be good, but even more, to avoid doing anything that made me look bad.

When I gave my heart to Jesus in my early thirties, I had no overwhelming emotional response, but I knew that something had changed inside me. I had experienced a heart change, something that became even more evident as the weeks went by. The problem was, this good news didn't immediately get to all the places in my heart. I knew in my mind, and to a degree in my heart, that I was now "clean, forgiven, washed, and accepted," but the deep and foundational lies that form destructive, toxic shame still needed to be dealt with.

So while I now had a perfect Father who loved, cherished, embraced, and accepted me no matter what, I still had to face the core shame that fought against this truth. Within me, a war was raging. I still had fear and anxiety, but now it related to my performance in my relationship with

God. I wanted God to be pleased with me, but even more, I wanted to avoid feeling that he was somehow *dis*pleased with or disappointed in me. Not until a couple of years later, when I submitted to the process of finding the wounded boy within me and bringing him to the Father, did this core shame get resolved. Theologically, the inner work I experienced is called *sanctification*.

Seeking Validation: "Will You Stamp My Ticket?"

When our core identity is shame-based rather than centered on the truth of who God has made us to be, we often struggle with the need for validation. At the most basic level, when something is valid, it is true. If something does not measure up or meet established criteria, then we would say it is invalid.

Over the years, we have worked with many men and women who have struggled with invalidation and their resultant lack of feeling okay with themselves. In some, this shows through their constant need for affirmation and approval. In others, it manifests through a hardened exterior, a wall—their way of trying to persuade themselves and those around them that they are legitimate, competent, or *somebody*. Either way, the most revealing symptom of invalidation is an inability to experience and maintain intimate relationships with others and with God.

A few years ago, during a time of personal ministry, the Lord dealt with my (Jerry's) heart about my struggle with invalidation. As I sought the Father for his insight, an image came to my mind. It was of me driving into a parking garage and receiving a ticket from the machine upon entering. A representative of the business I was visiting subsequently stamped the ticket for me, and I presented it to the attendant later upon exiting the garage. My validated ticket meant I was approved and therefore didn't have to pay.

I knew immediately what the Lord was showing me. One of my struggles in life has been to know that I am truly valid—that in my deepest part, I'm okay. This was particularly evident many years ago. Without realizing it, I frequently had my ticket out, hoping that someone would validate it to make me feel that I was alright. Not until I came to be a believer in Christ did he begin to reveal the power of invalidation in my life.

I am grateful for the profound work that God has done in this area over the years; yet during that personal ministry time, he revealed my need for an even deeper level of healing. I no longer held my ticket in my hand, but I did have it tucked away in my pocket. And in some circumstances—a disappointment, for instance, or a personal failure—I could still find that ticket and be tempted to hold it out for external validation.

This revelation helped me to submit my heart to God for further healing. I felt pain at the time, but today I no longer have a ticket to be stamped. Even better, the Father showed me that his stamp was already on me—VALID.

The Causes of Toxic Shame

As mentioned, our core identity—how we see and feel about ourselves—is formed very early. Various circumstances affect its development, but it is most significantly influenced by our primary caregivers, typically our father and mother, and also by teachers, siblings, and others who have a significant impact on us in childhood.

As children, we may be exposed to shaming messages that have a profound effect on us later in life.[27] These messages may be spoken to us, but they may also be communicated without words. They are simply learned in the environment. For example, your parents may never have told you, "Don't cry," but somehow you learned that crying was not a good thing to do in your home. Maybe you knew that crying would give your mother or father a reason to "really give you something to cry about."

These unspoken shaming messages can be transmitted through a glance, a frown, a stare, a gesture, a kick, or a slap in the face. My (Denise's) grandmother used to "bing" my cousins in the forehead with a spoon. Any of these actions can convey the same message of shame, which the child may internalize as being true about her very being.

Of course words, too, have a powerful impact. Shaming statements that children commonly hear include these: Shame on you. You should know better. How stupid can you be? Children are to be seen and not heard. Don't ask questions, just do as I say. Big boys/girls don't cry. That didn't hurt. You need to always look good. Don't betray the family. You'll never amount to anything.

The Polish side of my (Denise's) family liked to use the German word *dummkopf* to get a shame message across. The synonyms are extensive: stupid, idiot, blockhead, dodo bird, dope, dumbbell, imbecile, dummy, dunce, nincompoop, and plenty more. Just remembering some of the times I was called a dummkopf evokes an old, familiar "I'm bad" feeling in my stomach. Other painful labels damage children just as badly: worthless, whore, loser, screw-up, mistake—just to name a few. These are difficult messages for anyone to overcome.

In addition, the *absence* of affirmation, acceptance, affection, protection, and a sense of belonging communicate an equally devaluing message to a child, from which a core of shame develops. Children need to *hear* the words "I love you." Children need to *feel* the affection and appropriate touch and nurture from their parents or caregivers. Children don't understand that when their parents withhold affection and affirmation or inflict any type of abuse, it reveals something sadly missing in the parents, not something hopelessly flawed in the child.

Keep in mind that we're talking about a belief system which solidifies between the ages of two and four. On top of that, our personality is firmly established by the age of seven. Negative issues can, of course, affect a child beyond these formative years, but for the most part, only traumatic events such as the death of a loved one, divorce, sexual abuse, and the like, will dramatically shape a child's personality after that.

The Impact of Shame in a Dysfunctional Family

When one or both parents harbor undealt-with toxic shame, it affects everyone in the family. A child who doesn't sense that his mother or father loves him experiences overwhelming rejection and emotional abandonment. To deal with this pain, the child will find ways to cope. Often he learns to shut down his emotions as well as his needs.

Children growing up in dysfunctional, shame-based families learn three cardinal rules: Don't talk. Don't trust. And don't feel. A child doesn't talk because there is no place where his thoughts, opinions, and interests will be listened to, understood, and validated. She doesn't trust because she learns that being vulnerable and opening up to others gets her hurt so she decides that she can safely trust no one but herself. And a child doesn't feel because feeling is too painful.

Children who grow up in dysfunctional environments often also learn three additional rules: Don't hope. Don't plan. And don't dream. These rules speak for themselves.

As children progress from childhood to adolescence to adulthood, the rules they operated under as children in order to survive remain in place. Automatic responses and reactions in relational situations do not just go away, even when an individual becomes a believer in Christ. The rules that govern a wounded heart block our ability to feel the love of God the Father as well as the love of others. Eventually, though, these emotional handicaps begin to take their toll. We come to a point where we need to reach out for help both to God and to the helpers he places in our path. At last, we begin to unlearn the core lies we have lived by. Our unhealthy patterns start breaking down, and we can move forward with our healing.

Kristen, a precious young woman, wrote the following letter to her younger self during her counseling weekend with us. We could feel the almost tangible healing love that the Father was pouring into her wounded, shamed self as she read aloud to us. It was a moment of transformation in her life story.

Dear little Kristen,

I am writing to you because I want to affirm you and validate things in you that never were [validated] before. I want to tell you that you are free to be you. You are fully accepted. You are not weird. You were not made to carry the burdens of others. Lay those down at the feet of Jesus. It is not your job to manage the anxiety in the room or to buffer the conflict. All you have to do is completely and fully be you.

Little one, it is good to cry, to share, to express. Don't quench that. You don't have to be strong for anyone. You have a Father in heaven who will be strong for you. You have been given the ability to think deeply and analyze. You are "not too much" for anyone. You are perfect the way you were made.

I am sorry that I have avoided you, rejected you, and denied you. I am sorry that I have never considered you before. You are so young and are starving to find your place in the world. Please know that you are perfect the way that you are and that you are not too much for me. You are beautiful, without flaw, lovely in fact. You have nothing to measure up to and nothing to prove to me. I love you, I love you, I love you.

Love,
Me

The Lies Shame Tells

As you may have surmised, distorted beliefs or lies about ourselves, others, and God lie at the core of toxic shame. As I (Jerry) began to realize the presence of shame in my own life, I had to deal with lies that were influencing me at a deep level. They and their resultant shame didn't start with anything I did—I was too young. They rode in as a result of wounds in my parents inflicted by their own families of origin. I didn't want to believe these lies, especially once I knew what Christ had done for me and how the Father viewed me. But my best efforts to refute them were often inadequate.

A key aspect of healing from toxic shame is identifying the lies that we operate from and coming against them with the truth of Scripture.[28]

This is just one aspect of dealing with toxic shame, but it is an important one. We ask our counselees to honestly assess what they believe about themselves in such categories as self-worth, rejection, sense of belonging, guilt, and physical and personality traits. Do any of the following statements apply to you?

I don't belong. I will always be on the outside looking in.

My feelings don't count. No one cares what I feel.

I am the problem. When something goes wrong, it is my fault.

No one will ever care about me just for me. If you knew the real me, you would reject me.

Even when I do my best, it is not good enough. I can never meet the standard.

I have to plan every day of my life. I can't relax.

I need to be passive in order to avoid conflict that risks other's disapproval of me.

I must wear a mask so that people won't see who I really am and reject me.

Other lies show up more in our relationships with others and with God. Do any of these apply to you?

I have to guard and hide my emotions.

I cannot give anyone the satisfaction of knowing they have hurt me.

The correct way to respond if someone offends me is to punish them by withdrawing or cutting them off.

My value is based totally on others' judgment about me.

If I let anyone get close to me, I may get my heart broken again, and I can't risk that.

I am out there all alone; no one will come to my rescue if I need help.

God loves other people more than he loves me.

No matter how much I try, I will never be able to please God.

You may already know in your mind that a given statement isn't true. But a rational, intelligent answer isn't what counts here. Rather, ask yourself, "Does my life follow in the direction of any of these lies, especially when I'm not doing well emotionally?" Stated another way, "Do I struggle on the inside with any of these unhealthy thoughts and feelings?"

IMPORTANT! As we address the lies at the base of toxic shame, remember that *we are not dealing only with emotional issues but with spiritual ones as well.* The lies that exist in our hearts form spiritual strongholds or arguments that set themselves up against the knowledge of God (2 Corinthians10:5). When we acknowledge these lies to the Father and speak his truth to our hearts—the message *he* wants us to believe—we take the first step in demolishing the stronghold those lies have had on us.

Yet while refuting the lie is important, it is not enough. We can address the problem logically, but a logical argument will not change the heart. If true healing is to occur, the love of the Father has to get to the places—often very young places—where the injury occurred.

During my sessions with a pastoral counselor many years ago, I (Jerry) became aware of lie-based, childhood wounds that drove my adult behaviors. It was a critical revelation. I wasn't just crazy; my problems existed for a reason, and knowing this brought me relief. It also gave me hope for healing. If these things were written about in emotional healing books, then I wasn't the only one with a problem, and people really did get healed.

But had I stopped with that knowledge alone, my deeper heart healing would not have occurred.

The Bible describes the complete healing process like this:

[Jesus] will ignite the kingdom life within you, a fire within you, the Holy Spirit within you, changing you from the inside out. He's going to clean house—make a clean sweep of your lives. He'll place everything *true* in its proper place before God; everything *false* he'll put out with the trash to be burned" (Matthew 3:11–12 MSG, emphasis added).

Quoting from the prophet Isaiah, the gospel of Luke reveals the blueprint for Jesus's transformation project in our hearts and lives:

Make the road (our destiny) smooth and straight (with the incredible good news that God is *with* us and *for* us)!
Every ditch (of our past) will be filled in (every lie removed and all shame covered by God's grace),
Every bump smoothed out (our fears leveled and trust established),
The detours (our sinful choices) straightened out (with a glimpse of our destiny before us),
All the ruts paved over (Jesus prepares a new way for our true selves—our child-of-God selves—to be reborn). (Luke 3:5–6 MSG, parentheses ours)

This is an appropriate place to share a follow-up report from one of our clients, Stacie, after a two-day counseling retreat that transformed her heart:

Shortly after my trip to see you all, I visited my dad and mom. My six-year-old daughter Kinsey was with me. I was surprised as to how emotionally hard it was to go home and be with my parents. I felt vulnerable and slightly pissed off. One evening while we were there, Kinsey was fiddling around with an old sheet on the floor. She was using it like skates and was gliding around dancing. My dad says to her, "What are you doing? What would make you do that to that sheet?"

Now normally, I would immediately get on to her, because she had upset my dad. However, I looked at my dad and I said to him, "Dad, she's not doing anything wrong. She is just doing what kids do—having fun." And do you know what he said to me? "Oh, OK."

That's it! That's all he said! What an amazing moment for me!

Lots of stuff rolled off with that one interchange! First of all,

I was able to defend Kinsey—which also means I was able to defend that little girl inside of me as well! Secondly, I'm excited that I was able to recognize that Kinsey was just being a kid and enjoying the freedom to play. This is an ongoing challenge for me, but I believe I am getting better at it.

After we got back from my parents house, I had another interesting experience with Kinsey. While we were riding in the car, we had a conversation about food. She doesn't like to eat her veggies, so I told her no dessert if she doesn't eat her veggies. As the conversation went on she started to cry and said to me, "I feel like a rotten egg. Nobody wants to eat me!"

Wow, that one took me for a loop. Immediately one of the messages on shame that I heard when I was at your place came back to me: "There is nothing you can ever do to make God love you less—nothing—N-O-T-H-I-N-G!" So I pulled over and stopped the car. I got out, went to Kinsey in the back seat and hugged her. I was able to tell her she is not a rotten egg and I would choose her! I would eat her up! (So silly I know!) Then, after a few more minutes of hugs, we continued on our way.

Stacie had previously shared with us that during the times when she needed to discipline Kinsey (who was already crying in advance), a part of her wanted to just hold Kinsey. But she felt that she needed to spank her because it was her job to teach her daughter about sin. Now she is seeing that what she needs to teach Kinsey most of all is about *love*.

How Shame Taints Our Relationship with God

Toxic shame exacts an exorbitant price in our lives. It costs us love, friendships, acceptance, hope, and connectedness. Worst of all, it robs us of an intimate relationship with God. Shame causes us to see the Father through distorted lenses and thus inhibits us from receiving the love he has for us. Instead of enjoying simply *being* with God as the overflow of a love relationship with him, we wind up performing for God in order to please him and earn his love. Then when we finally get burned out or depressed, we complain, "I did all these things for God and got no reward. He must be disappointed with me."

Shame keeps us locked in this mentality and fruitless cycle. In our daily walk with God, we find ourselves comparing other people's blessings and gifts to ours; their healing to ours; the fruit of their work to ours. We see others as having God's favor, but not ourselves. Others get the words and help from God that we wanted; they experience the love of God in more manifest ways than us. We feel rejected, abandoned, worthless, alone, ashamed, and beaten down. The core message haunts us: *There must be something inherently wrong with me that God doesn't hear me, see me, speak to me, touch me, or bless me.*

A Moment of Reflection

In closing this chapter, we would like to share a powerful poem that we have adapted for use in counseling. It brings home the power of what we have been describing in this chapter. The stark truth in the last verse hits especially hard: destructive shame robs our identity and thwarts our destiny.

MY NAME IS TOXIC SHAME

I was there at your conception.
You felt me in the fluid of your mother's womb.
I came upon you before you could speak—
Before you understood,
Before you had any way of knowing.
I came upon you when you were learning to walk—
When you were unprotected and exposed,
When you were vulnerable and needy,
Before you had any boundaries.
My name is Toxic Shame.

I came upon you before you could know I was there.
I severed your soul.
I pierced you to the core.
I brought you feelings of being flawed and defective.
I brought you feelings of distrust, ugliness, stupidity, doubt—
Feelings of worthlessness, inferiority, and unworthiness.
I made you feel different.
I told you, "There is something wrong with you."
I soiled your godlikeness.
My name is Toxic Shame.

I am the internal voice that whispers words of condemnation.
I live in secrecy—
In the deep darkness of depression and despair and loneliness.
I sneak up on you.
I catch you off guard.
I come through the back door,
Uninvited, unwanted.
I am the first to arrive to tell you, "You'll never measure up.
You'll never belong."
My name is Toxic Shame.

I come from caretakers who abandon, ridicule, abuse, neglect,
reject, and ignore.
I am empowered by the shocking intensity of a parent's criticism,
The cruel remarks of siblings,
The jeering humiliation of other children,
Your awkward reflection in the mirror,
The touch that feels icky and frightening,
The slap, the pinch, the pointing finger that ruptures trust.
I make you feel hopeless,
Like there is no way out.
My name is Toxic Shame.

My pain is so unbearable that you must pass me on to others
Through control, perfectionism, contempt, criticism, blame,
envy, judgment, power, and rage.
My pain is so intense,
You must cover me up with masks, addictions, performance,
rigid roles, anger, defenses, and religion.
I twist who you are into what you do and have.
I murder your soul and you pass me on for generations.
I destroy your identity.
I erase your destiny.
My name is Toxic Shame.[29]

PRAYER

Father, I want to be whole. I want to view myself the way you view me and love myself the way you love me. Lord, if there is any destructive, toxic shame within me that hinders my ability to do so, I ask you to reveal it to me. I ask this so that I can ultimately walk in the freedom that you desired for me when you sent your Son Jesus in order to restore all things—including me.

I want to be free of the lies that still affect me and influence my ability to love you, myself, and others. And I know that if you reveal this type of shame in me, it is already your plan to ultimately heal me from its effects. Please have your way in me. Thank you for your love. I ask all of this in the name of your Son, Jesus, amen.

QUESTIONS FOR REFLECTION

1. Review the questions in the section on "Faces of Toxic Shame." To which questions did you answer yes? Did you previously relate these symptoms to toxic shame?

2. How do you describe the difference between healthy shame and toxic shame?

3. Shaming messages can be spoken as well as silently communicated through a look, a gesture, or a frown. What shaming messages do you remember from growing up? Are there any messages you internalized that we have not included?

4. In the section on "The Lies Shame Tells," which statements reflect the way you feel or what you heard? How would your life be different if those lies were silenced?

5. How has toxic shame affected your relationship with God?

6. Reread the poem, "My Name Is Toxic Shame." How do the faces of shame that it describes affect you? You may want to record some of your thoughts in your journal.

7. Ask the Father to heal your identity and restore your destiny—the destiny he knit together in your mother's womb.

8. Pray the closing prayer from your heart.

CHAPTER NINE

GOOD GRIEF:
FROM SELF-FORGIVENESS
TO SELF-ACCEPTANCE

When I invited Jesus into my life, I thought he was going
to put up some wallpaper and hang a few pictures. But he
started knocking out walls and adding on rooms.
I said, "I was expecting a nice cottage." But he said,
"I'm making a palace in which to live."
—C. S. Lewis

When you forgive yourself, you rewrite your script.
What you are in your present scene is not tied down to what
you did in an earlier scene. The bad guy you played in Act
One is eliminated and you play Act Two as a good guy.
—Lewis Smedes

Grief Says, "It Matters"

Loss is an inevitable part of life. At one time or another we all experience
it. Our losses can either hinder our growth and destiny or help us move
forward to fulfillment. In order for us to heal from our past wounds, we
must be able to grieve over our losses.

You may ask, "Why should I have to grieve? Being healed should bring joy and gladness, not sadness and grief." Yes, joy, gladness, and gratitude are important end products of being healed, and you will experience them at times on the healing journey. But being able to grieve is still vital.

Two of our favorite sayings express this truth: "You must grieve it to leave it," and, "You can't fully heal what you can't really feel." When you allow yourself to feel sorrow or sadness as a result of a loss, you are assigning value to that loss. You are saying that it mattered.

Grieving losses, especially significant ones, is normal. If you don't or won't, you will have difficulty coming to a place of acceptance and embracing what is in store for your future. Your heart will be adversely affected.

On the other hand, effective, godly grieving leads to acceptance of yourself, of others, and of your past. It also allows you to break free from unhealthy patterns of relating that can be bound to unresolved pain.

I (Jerry) have had a very difficult time grieving the losses in my life. Not until I was around thirty-six years old did I realize what loss really was, and that grieving it was not only alright, but necessary. Although I had experienced different losses up to that point, what finally helped me to grieve was God allowing me to see the impact of my early childhood wounds. I hadn't received things that I needed; I had, however, received things that I didn't need; and both sides of that equation were important to me and also to God. As I stopped denying and minimizing my past and allowed grief to occur, I was able to at long last *feel* the impact of my losses.

One of the challenges in grieving can be the wounds themselves. If you learn as a child that it's better not to feel unpleasant feelings, and if you move on quickly when bad things happen, then you maintain the same pattern as you get older unless something intervenes to change it. In my case, that "something" was the Holy Spirit. When I was thirty-three years old, he moved into my "heart house" and began to move some things out and bring new things in. He did what he does for everyone who places their trust in him: he gave me a *new heart* (Ezekiel 36:26). And in so doing, he let me begin to see and feel things from *his* perspective. From his heart. He showed me that I mattered, and therefore what had happened to me as a child also mattered. And because it mattered to him, it should also matter to me. When I allowed him to show me *why* it mattered—the cost—I could at last begin to grieve.

Understanding the Grief Process

In her classic book *On Death and Dying,*[30] Elisabeth Kubler-Ross identifies five distinct stages of grief:

- *Denial* ("This isn't happening to me." "I can't believe it.")
- *Anger* ("Why is this happening to me?" "That isn't fair." "That was wrong.")
- *Bargaining* ("I promise I'll be a better person if _____." "If only you'll _____, then I'll _____.")
- *Sadness* ("I lost something of value." "It hurts." "It matters.") or *Depression* ("I just don't care anymore." "I can't fight this anymore.")
- *Acceptance* ("I'm ready for whatever comes." "There is still more for me for the future.")

Grief is not a clean process; it can be quite messy. It is a tangled ball of emotions—anxiety, sadness, confusion, disappointment, guilt, fear, anger, emptiness, denial, helplessness, depression, apathy, dread, and numbness, to name a few. We can go in and out of these feelings quickly at times. We can also get stuck in one of them. Grief is not linear; it does not proceed neatly from one stage to the next. Instead, we may move back and forth between two or more stages before finally reaching acceptance.

The extent of our grief also varies depending on the perceived magnitude of our loss. For example, the grief of losing an elderly parent will likely be different from that of the sudden death of a child. Also, the time it takes to grieve varies for every person; there is no magic number like six months or a year.

Finally, even when we have effectively grieved a loss, that doesn't mean we will never feel pain when we think of that loss in the future.

However, the intensity of our emotions will be much less and should not affect how we function, as can happen during early and intense grief over a major loss.

Is Grieving Biblical?

The act of grieving—also called mourning in the Bible—features prominently in both the Old and New Testaments. The Old Testament makes various references to grief, both people's and God's. God grieved over the sinfulness and rebellion of humankind (Genesis 6:6–7; Isaiah 63:10). Many of the Psalms express the lament of God's people (see Psalms 13, 42, and 43 as examples).

In the New Testament in Mark 3:5, the NKJV says that Jesus was "grieved" by the hardness of heart in those who opposed his healing on the Sabbath. In Luke 19:41, as Jesus approached Jerusalem, he wept over the city, knowing the cost its people would incur for failing to recognize and respond to him and his message of life. When he saw Mary and others weeping at the tomb of Lazarus, Jesus was "deeply moved in spirit and troubled" (John 11:33); and mere minutes before he raised Lazarus from the dead, "Jesus wept" (John 11:35).

In Matthew 5:4, Jesus included the topic of mourning in the Beatitudes when He said, "Blessed are those who mourn, for they will be comforted." And in Romans 12:15, Paul exhorts us to "Rejoice with those who rejoice; mourn with those who mourn."

How God Met Me in My Grief: A Personal Story

It was the day after I (Denise) had lost our only child to a miscarriage, and I was in the first stages of grief: numb, questioning God, and not believing what had just happened. The phone rang and I answered it. On the other end was a woman, sobbing. After several minutes, I realized it was my oldest sister. She couldn't even talk—she just wept. And I wept along with her.

What a gift from God her phone call was to me that day! At that moment, my sister was the heart of God to me. You see, God weeps when I weep. I love that about God. Psalm 56:8 NLT says, "You [God] keep track of all my sorrows. You have collected all my tears in your bottle. You have recorded each one in your book."

After losing the baby, I also received other calls rejoicing that my child was in heaven. These people rejoiced while I was mourning. I felt wounded and more alone, misunderstood and judged by them. Later, I had to forgive them from the hurt and release them.

Many times after losing our baby, I asked God, *Why?* I was like a petulant child repeatedly demanding to know, "Why? Why? Why?" But I didn't really want to understand; I wanted God to change my barrenness. Later in my healing, I took God off my hook and asked him to forgive me. He showed me that there was no explanation he could ever give me that would satisfy my "Why?" So I learned to live with the mystery of God, and along the way I learned acceptance.

Why Grieving Childhood Wounds Is So Important

Grieving wounds incurred in childhood may seem less important than grieving a loved one's death. But doing so is essential for healing. When we pray with our clients in this area, we ask God that the grief be "no more or no less than is necessary."

People's desire to experience the fullness of Jesus's intervention in the healing process can sometimes cause them to over-spiritualize what occurs and bypass the necessary grieving. For example, someone who seeks inner-healing prayer might experience the Holy Spirit moving in a significant way. The person has a genuine encounter with Jesus, revealing himself in the midst of a painful childhood memory. As a result, the person receives a great measure of healing. One might conclude that as a result of the prayer time, the person has been fully healed.

But when this conclusion is reached prematurely and the process of grieving is bypassed, deep healing—and the fruit of a changed heart—may not occur. Grieving is even more overlooked when childhood wounds result from acts of omission—a lack of love, affection, and guidance—versus acts of commission such as verbal, physical, and sexual abuse.

During my personal healing journey, I (Jerry) experienced times when God "broke in" during healing prayer. Those encounters were important parts of the process, and I am grateful for them, both to God and to those who facilitated them. But connecting with my pain and allowing the grief to come was still essential. Had I not done so, the healing of my heart would not have been as effective.

Anger as a Pointer

Anger is an important emotion in the grieving process as well as in life. However, it is often misunderstood and mismanaged. Many people who are angry inside may either deny their anger or attempt to minimize or rationalize it. But suppressing anger only inhibits and delays the healing process.

Is it biblical to express anger? Scripture cautions us against sinful, destructive anger and abounds with examples of such anger. Yet many other places in the Bible, especially the Psalms, demonstrate appropriate anger (see, for instance, Psalms 69 and 109). The prophet, Jeremiah, openly expressed his anger with God (Jeremiah 20:7–18). Jesus displayed great anger when he cleansed the temple, but he did not sin (John 2:13–16). Paul the apostle clearly tells us to be angry but to avoid sinning in our anger (Ephesians 4:26).

While anger can become destructive and take on a life of its own, it often serves simply as a pointer to deeper emotions of pain, fear, and disappointment that are rooted in our wounds. Whether those wounds came during childhood or later in life's journey, they result in feeling betrayed, rejected, abandoned, unaccepted, insecure, or inadequate. Authentic anger is a passionate feeling which tells us that something matters—and these emotions matter. Anger is often what guides us to the source of our pain, where the Father desires to bring healing.

God Will Meet Us in Our Pain and Anger

On a number of occasions with our clients, God has revealed his presence in surprising ways. We were working with a woman who was processing tremendous pain from childhood sexual abuse by her father as well as deep hurts from others. In preparation for a particular session, we asked her to make a list of people from her past whom she needed to forgive. As the session commenced, she began to forgive her father for his abuse. She became angrier and angrier—and her focus shifted from her earthly father to God. She told him how mad she was at him for not protecting her or caring about her.

When our client's anger with God was most intense, as her rage mixed with tears, the presence of the Lord entered the counseling room. All three of us were overwhelmed; it was a hold-your-breath, awesome moment. The Father came and poured out his compassionate love on his angry, brokenhearted daughter, who melted instantly in his presence. The three of us were in tears as she described how God came, put his arms around her, and held her.

Some of my (Jerry's) most intimate times with God have occurred during the most painful, broken parts of my healing journey. Often I was in a place of anger—anger at others, and sometimes, anger at God for not having been there to help me. Having had an angry father caused me to reject anger altogether. Yet anger still festered inside me and needed to be dealt with, and God initiated the process.

God isn't concerned so much about anger itself as long as we don't hurt ourselves or others with it. He is more concerned with revealing and healing anger's underlying causes. We must invite him into our pain—and our anger—and allow him to do what he does best: heal the brokenhearted and set the captives free.

The Forgiveness Process: Assessing the Cost

Grieving is not only important in processing loss. It is also essential to the process of forgiveness. When we grieve, we become aware of what the loss cost us. In the case of childhood wounding, we reaped the consequences of not receiving what we needed or receiving things that were damaging to us.

Truly forgiving from our hearts requires us to connect with the impact of sins done to us or by us. As Neil Anderson says in *Ministering the Steps to Freedom in Christ*,[31] "You allow God to bring to the surface the painful emotions you feel towards those who have hurt you." For this reason, we normally will not lead a client to forgive others early in the healing process. For most clients, the *desire* to forgive already exists in their hearts, and God knows that. But there's more to forgiveness than simply saying that we forgive. Our words of forgiveness have to be prayed with *heart meaning*.

When we ask a client, "What did this wound cost you?" we're asking that he look not only at its impact on him as a child, but also at what it has cost him in the years that followed: Failed relationships. Divorce. Problems in the workplace. Difficulty connecting with God. Addictive struggles. Wounding his own children. Or perhaps simply not being able to live life the way God intended.

We're not implying that others are responsible for one's sinful responses to past wounding. Rather, we're pointing out that those wounds can set a person on an unhealthy path that inclines him toward a particular sin or struggle.

When we assist our clients through the forgiveness process, we emphasize that Jesus himself was well aware of the cost of others' sin against him. It was from the cross and his deepest pain that he spoke the words, "Father, forgive them, for they do not know what they are doing" (Luke 23:34). If a client cannot connect emotionally to their own cost, we don't necessarily wait to initiate the work of forgiveness. However, we do realize that a time of greater emotional connection may come in the future, and forgiveness will then need to be revisited.

When we walk a client through forgiveness, we ask them to verbalize, naming the person being forgiven, his or her sin, and its impact, thus: "I forgive you, _____, for _____. It made me feel _____." We ask the client to be as specific as possible rather than offering a generic, blanket-type of forgiveness. For example, a client might say something like, "I forgive you, Dad, for being gone all the time and not being there when I was growing up. This made me feel unwanted, of no value, rejected, not special.…" We might also have the person add, "From this place, I choose to forgive you and I release you."

Bear in mind that the forgiveness process we have shared here is an act done between the client and God. We are merely facilitators.

Self-Forgiveness: A Key to Loving and Forgiving Others

The need for self-forgiveness and the self-acceptance that follows is often more powerful than the need to forgive others. However, it often slips under the radar of our self-awareness.

The basis for this book is that in order to truly love others, I must be able and willing to love myself. Self-forgiveness is similar. If I want to forgive others, then I must be able and willing to forgive myself. Jesus said, "Love others as well [in the same manner] as you love yourself" (Mark 12:31 MSG). If I don't love myself, but rather am hard on myself, it's like rewording what Jesus said to read, "Be as hard on others as you are on yourself." Or, "Hate others as you hate yourself." Or, "Show no grace to others as you show no grace to yourself."

It is amazing how hard people are on themselves. Often we will ask a client, "If you felt hatred or loathing for another person, would that be a problem for you?" Usually the answer is, "Of course. I would feel bad about it, and I would work on forgiving that person and dealing with any resentment I felt toward them." Our next question is, "Why do you treat yourself any differently? Does God view your hatred toward others as unacceptable but your self-contempt as acceptable?"

You might be thinking, "Okay, I get the point." But somehow we really *don't* get it. How we see and feel about ourselves is much more than an emotional issue—it is a spiritual one. And it will interfere with our ability to love God and live in freedom.

Brennan Manning, in his book, *The Signature of Jesus*, told of his own need for self-acceptance. He was en route from Florida to Iowa when his plane got rerouted to Kansas City due to bad weather. Here is what he shared:

> I was wandering around the terminal in my clerical collar, when a man approached me and asked if he could make his confession. We sat down in the relative privacy of the Delta Crown Room and he began. His life had been scarred with serious sin. Midway through, he started to cry. Embracing him I found myself in tears, reassuring him of the joy in the kingdom over the return of a repentant sinner and reminding him that the Prodigal Son experienced an intimacy with his father that his sinless, self-righteous brother never knew.
>
> The man's face was transfigured. The merciful love of the redeeming God broke through his guilt and self-hatred. I prayed a prayer of thanksgiving for the Lord's unbearable forgiveness, infinite patience, and tender love. The man wept for joy. As we parted, he glowed with the radiance of a saved sinner.
>
> As I fastened my seatbelt in the DC-10, I heard an inner voice like a bell clanging deep in my soul: *Brennan, would you do for yourself what you have just done for your brother? Would you so eagerly and enthusiastically forgive yourself, accept yourself, and love yourself?*[32]

In his book *Total Forgiveness*, R. T. Kendall states that "grace isn't grace if we have to be good enough for it to apply to us." Here is what he shares regarding forgiveness of self:

> Moses had a past. He was a murderer. (See Exodus 2:11–12.) But years later he would proclaim the eighth commandment: "You shall not murder" (Exod. 20:13). David had a past, but he also had a future after his shame: "Then I will teach transgressors your

ways, and sinners will turn back to you," he wrote (Ps. 51:13). Jonah deliberately ran from God, but he was still used in an astonishing revival (Jon. 3). Peter's disgrace—denying Jesus—did not abort God's plans for him. But all these men had to forgive themselves before they could move into the ministry God had planned for them.[33]

As we help our clients connect with their childhood wounds and extend forgiveness as needed, they often have to deal with their own sinful responses to the hurts they received. Frequently they realize more clearly where they have wounded their own children. In some cases, they may be led to go to their children (who often are now adults), acknowledge sorrow over how they hurt them, and ask them for forgiveness. In order to do this from the heart, clients must be able to know—really know—that they themselves have been forgiven by God and are totally accepted by him; and they must have truly forgiven themselves as well. If self-forgiveness is still being worked on and has not been settled in a client's heart, it is usually best to wait a little longer before seeking forgiveness from others. Otherwise, the forgiveness a person seeks from others may unknowingly be self-seeking, motivated by a desire to feel more self-forgiveness.

When we are able to feel the impact of sin—not only what has been done against us, but also what we ourselves have done or failed to do— then we will also be able to feel some of God's grief. We experience what Paul referred to as a "godly sorrow that leads to repentance [life-giving change]" (2 Corinthians 7:10). By allowing the Father to take us through this process, always remembering who we are in him, we will ultimately come to a place of self-acceptance.

However, if toxic shame and self-contempt retain a strong grip on us, we will not arrive at self-acceptance; instead, we will end up stuck in an ungodly, worldly sorrow that leads to death (2 Corinthians 7:10).So we do well to remember what God's primary purpose is when we deal with the issue of loving, forgiving, and accepting ourselves: He desires more of our hearts. He wants our hearts to be available to receive his love and love him in return, and then be able to love others. If anything is taking us in the opposite direction, then we need to stop and ask God to redirect us to what is truly from him and ultimately brings life.

A Prayer for Self-Forgiveness

If you find it hard to fully forgive, release, and embrace yourself the way God does, try praying the following prayer:

> *Lord, I thank you that I am so very special to you and that you freely forgive me and choose to no longer remember my sins or the ways in which I fail to love as you love. As you freely extend mercy to me, I also choose to apply this same mercy to myself. I choose to forgive myself and to no longer hold myself in judgment or contempt. I choose to release myself just as you release me. Help me to believe and speak the truth about myself that you have spoken and have confirmed in your Word. I choose to embrace myself the way you embrace me.*
> *Thank you for this gift that comes from your heart. Amen.*

Accepting Yourself the Way God Accepts You

As we take all that has happened to us, grieve its impact, and move through the process of forgiving others and ourselves, we become ready to accomplish the final step: acceptance. But in the case of learning to love ourselves, we not only have to come to the place of accepting what has happened to us—we also have to come to the place of accepting ourselves. Without reaching this final step, we remain in emotional and spiritual conflict, because we are not in agreement with what God says about us.

James Bryan Smith, author of *Embracing the Love of God*, describes self-acceptance this way:

> God has chosen to accept what we deem unacceptable. The parts of us that cause us shame do not shame God. Here is the Good

News: even if we feel condemned by our own hearts, God is greater than our hearts…

God's acceptance should lead us to self-acceptance. Grace heals our shame not by trying to find something good and lovely within us that is worth loving, but by looking at us as we are, the good and the bad, the lovely and the unlovely, and simply accepting us. God accepts us with the promise that we will never be unacceptable to him. Now it is ours to do the same for ourselves.[34]

John the apostle encourages us with these words:

My dear children, let's not just talk about love; let's practice real love. This is the only way we'll know we're living truly, living in God's reality. It's also the way to *shut down debilitating self-criticism,* even when there is something to it. For God is greater than our worried hearts and knows more about us than we do ourselves. And friends, once that's taken care of and we're *no longer accusing or condemning ourselves,* we're bold and free before God! We're able to stretch our hands out and receive what we asked for because we're doing what he said, doing what pleases him [which includes accepting ourselves] (1 John 3:18–21 MSG, emphases added).

In his book *On Loving God*, St. Bernard of Clairvaux describes Christian maturity as the stage where "we love ourselves for God's sake."[35] This means that if God says we are a jewel in his crown—we are. If God says we are the apple of his eye—we are. If God says we are loved, lovely, and lovable—we are. If God calls us his beloved—guess what? We are. Accepting ourselves honors God and puts him back on the throne—the all-knowing, omnipotent, righteous, and passionate King.

A Letter to the Child Within

Dear younger Conner,

I want you to know you're not a disappointment and that you're not in need of change, that you are acceptable right now just as you are. I saw a picture of you in my heart's eye the other day. I saw a pile of mud and crap and knew that you were underneath, just waiting to be rescued. Younger Conner, I want you to know I am going to dig you out—I'm going to find you and the Lord will set you free. I'm not ashamed of you and I'm not ashamed of who you have become. The Father is going to tell us who we are and we will walk free. You're going to be an even better husband, a wonderful father and a lover of God. Just you wait—you will see—because God has promised to never do anything to you but good, even when circumstances look choppy.

I am no longer afraid to say I love you and I am confident to tell you we will make it. I'm proud of you and who you have become. And I am beginning to understand who I am in Christ and in God.

The adult Conner

A Declaration of Self-Acceptance

We invite you to embrace the following declaration of who you are. Read it aloud and remember that what you are reading is in full agreement with what God says about you.

I am me. I am made in the very image of God, just a little lower than the angels. I am unique. In the entire world there is no one exactly like me. This means that I am important to God.

I can accept myself because God accepts me. I can love myself because God loves me. I know that I matter because God sent his Son, Jesus Christ, and through him he gave me the chance to live abundantly and eternally.

I do not have to be perfect in order to be loved, because God loves me as I am—imperfect. This means that I am important even when I have rough edges in my life and when I make mistakes, even big ones. I can fail. I can stumble. God still says, "I love you!" I don't have to have everything in the right order or have everything cleaned up for God to accept me. And in knowing this, I can live with myself. I have hope that I can take all that I am and all that I have to God—the good and the bad—and he will keep on helping me grow more and more into his image.

I can be totally honest. I can be my child-of-God self. I look forward to the plans he has for me. With his help and guidance, I will become a reflection of his love and acceptance toward myself and others.

So I accept the fact that I am important, that I have value and worth. I have eternal value. I love myself and I like myself, every part, because I choose to love who he loves—and that is me.

A Final Thought: Increase In Order to Decrease

As the wounded younger child within us increases and is acknowledged, loved, forgiven, and accepted, so also the grown-up child can now be unified and loved by us. As a result, our God-given, true identity is able to come forth. And when this happens, something very interesting begins to take place: our adult self, who now has a self to give, can choose to *decrease*—to prefer and bless others and lay down our life for others. In other words, the presence of God flows—indeed, overflows—from us freely. We love more. We love God, love self, and love others—the ultimate goal.

P R A Y E R

Lord Jesus, I want to be able to grieve what has also grieved your heart. I want to be able to live from a heart that is connected to you and to life and not simply step over things in my past that have been difficult and painful. You did not design me to be able to stockpile losses, whether childhood losses or losses as an adult. You desire that I feel what you feel and that I work through my losses rather than sidestep them. I need your help in doing this. I need to know that you will be with me as I allow you to help me "grieve it to leave it."

I also need your help in order to forgive others as well as myself and come to a place of acceptance—not resignation, but true acceptance. Lord, help me to accept myself the way you accept me. Help me to truly love what you love—me. In your name, amen.

QUESTIONS FOR REFLECTION

1. When you were growing up, what did you do with unpleasant feelings when bad things happened? How do you process hurt and loss today? Has the pattern changed?

2. In the process of forgiveness, we believe it is important to ask the Holy Spirit to search our heart rather than searching it ourselves. This allows us to avoid being hard on ourselves and holding ourselves in contempt. When you are ready to walk through forgiveness, use the format from the section on "The Forgiveness Process."

3. If you want to forgive, accept, and love others, then you must be willing to forgive, accept, and love yourself. Which is harder for you? Take a few moments and pray the "Prayer for Self-Forgiveness." Even if you have to pray it several times to let its truth sink in, take a first step today to acknowledge that you want to agree with God and forgive yourself.

4. Write a letter of acceptance to the child within you. Include what you have been learning and how you see and feel about this part of you.

5. Reread the closing prayer. Imagine and believe that the Father is standing right next to you with his arm around you, partnering with you to heal your heart.

CHAPTER TEN

AMAZING GRACE: THE TOO-GOOD-TO-BE-TRUE GOOD NEWS

I used up all my energy trying hard to outperform the jerk that I know I am inside.
—A young man struggling with self-hatred

In our profession, the issue of grace comes up over and over again. It has become overwhelmingly obvious to us that many true, God-loving believers either do not understand the true meaning of grace or else they have personally disqualified themselves from receiving it. Either way, they fail to experience the reality of the gospel—the too-good-to-be-true good news that came when Jesus arrived in our lives.

What Grace Really Means

Let's examine this word grace more closely. According to *Nelson's Bible Dictionary*, grace refers to "a favor or kindness shown without regard or merit of the one who receives it and in spite of what that same person deserves."[36] Think of the times you have extended grace to a spouse, family member, friend, or coworker, and that person didn't do anything to earn it. In fact, the very act of your extending grace implies that it wasn't deserved.

The Greek word for grace in the New Testament is *charis*. According to *Vine's Expository Dictionary of Biblical Words*, grace is "the friendly disposition from which the kind act proceeds—with graciousness, loving-kindness, goodwill—especially with reference to the divine favor [of God]."[37] God offers grace to us as a gift through his Son, Jesus, who is described as being "full of grace" (John 1:14). Grace does not depend on anything we can do to earn it nor anything we could do to lose it (Ephesians 2:8–9). It is a free, universal, spontaneous gift, and it brings forth a sense or feeling of pleasure, joy, and gratitude in the one who receives it.

When was the last time you actually felt joy as a result of the kindness and favor of the Father toward you? When was the last time that pleasure or gratitude simply rose up in your heart as a result of the Father's grace flowing toward you? If it was recently and happens frequently, that's great—but if not, keep reading.

One of our clients shared a perfect example of this free, spontaneous gift. She had been dealing with her seventeen-year-old daughter about following the guidelines established for using her car. One was that the daughter needed to be home by a certain time during the week when school was in session. If she violated this rule, she would not be allowed to drive to school the following day.

Naturally, the daughter came in late, and the next morning her mother forbade her to use her car for school or anything else that day. Her daughter was upset with her mom and continued to pout and push back. But her mom stuck with the boundary, reminding her daughter that this consequence had been clearly communicated to her and thus was her own choice.

Then the woman heard the Lord speak to her heart, "Give her the keys and let her take her car. This time extend grace." After pondering this for a few minutes, she went to her daughter and handed her the keys. Her daughter immediately burst into tears. This free gift of grace when she didn't deserve it penetrated the young woman's heart in a profound way. In this particular situation, the right thing to do—enforce an appropriate boundary—got trumped by the best thing to do, namely, teach the daughter about grace. It also emphasized the importance of relying on God and trusting that we can hear from his heart rather than simply relying on the predetermined plan. The Lord used this situation to take our client as well as her daughter further into his heart of grace.

I Am a New Creation

The root of the word *transformation* is from the Greek word *metamorphoo*, which means, "to change from the inside out." This is where we get the word *metamorphosis.*

In nature, God has shown us a profound example of transformation and metamorphosis in the life cycle of the butterfly. The butterfly begins as a crawling caterpillar. But at some point, it sequesters itself in a safe location, becomes very still, and weaves itself into a pupa or cocoon. Then, in this place of hiding, the caterpillar's old form dies and liquefies. Everything it has been and known dissolves. What once was, is no more. The same chemical substance exists, but not in the same form; it is being re-formed in secrecy, and the creature that eventually breaks forth from the pupa bears no resemblance to what it once was. The liquid mess has been transformed into a beautiful butterfly which neither looks nor acts like its previous caterpillar nature. It no longer crawls—it flies!

Now, if God sat down with the caterpillar and said, "I have made you to be a butterfly—I have created you to fly," the caterpillar might say, "But look at me. This is who I am. I could try harder to be a better caterpillar and learn to crawl faster. But grow wings and fly? I don't think so!" Flying for a caterpillar doesn't come through increased effort. It comes through transformation.

That is exactly the awesome miracle that occurs when we become new creatures in Christ! God doesn't stop at merely saving us from judgment; he *changes us* into something we were not before. He transforms us, fashioning in us a brand-new nature and identity capable of fulfilling the destiny he has woven into us. The Father longs to turn our "old mess" into his glory. He wants to draw us to somewhere safe where we can be still and know that he is God our Father, who will transform us—no longer to crawl, but to soar!

Continuing with the butterfly analogy, we like how James Bryan Smith addresses us as a new creation in his book *The Good and Beautiful God*:

> …[The caterpillar, a worm,] goes into a cocoon—a chrysalis, in which the root word, appropriately, is "Christ." And it emerges a butterfly, completely transformed. The old has passed. The new has arrived. It was once weighed down by gravity; now it can fly. Christians were once under the reign of sin, but now we can live in freedom.
>
> And you can also see why it's so painful to me that so many Christians don't understand this? When I hear a Christian say, "I'm just a sinner saved by grace," I want to say, "That makes as much sense as a butterfly saying, 'I'm just a worm with wings.'"[38]

The bottom line is this: *As a believer in Christ, we are not defined by our sin or our struggle.*

Yes, we struggle and we sin, but our core identity—who we really are—has been transformed. *We are not sinners who have been forgiven* (as important as God's forgiveness is!), but *lovers of God who have a good and redeemed nature.* And if our true identity has been redeemed, then our heart is not sinful but righteous.

Our heart is good.

If we do not internalize this truth, we will always focus on getting better and sinning less instead of resting in the love of Father God and allowing his kindness to lead us toward change (Romans 2:4).

Our core identity is now righteous—a saint, a butterfly—no matter what I do or do not do. And this true identity is not based on ourselves but on placing our faith in Christ and what he has accomplished through his death and resurrection (Romans 4:24, Philippians 3:9). Who we really are—our identity and our position as it relates to God—has been changed.

Like the caterpillar, we need to allow God to transform us from the inside out into who we were truly created to be. Then we can say, from the heart, "I am me and I am very okay! I was made to fly."

Servanthood to Sonship

Many of us Christians live in a master–servant relationship with God, a "just tell me what to do and I'll do it" relationship.

You might think, "That's what I want—for God to just tell me what to do." But would that work for you with your spouse or best friend? Not many warm fuzzies in that kind of relationship, are there?

If God is your Father and you are his child, how much more rewarding and meaningful would a relationship be in which he invited you to walk with and partner with him rather than just giving you orders? Wouldn't that feel a lot closer than a master?

Let's look at a day in the life of a servant versus a son and see what the differences are:

The servant is accepted and appreciated on the basis of *what he does*, the child on the basis of *who he is*.

The servant starts the day *anxious and worried*, wondering if his work will really please his master. The child *rests in the secure love* of his family.

The servant is accepted because of his *workmanship*, the son or daughter because of a *relationship*.

The servant is accepted because of his *productivity and performance*. The child belongs because of his *position as a person*.

At the end of the day, the servant has peace of mind only if he is sure he has *proven his worth by his work. The next morning his anxiety begins again.* The child can be *secure all day, and know that tomorrow won't change his status.*

When a servant *fails, his whole position is a stake;* he might lose his job. When a child fails, he will be grieved because he has hurt his parents, and he will be corrected and disciplined. But *he is not afraid of being thrown out. His basic confidence is in belonging and being loved, and his performance does not change the stability of his position.*[39]

Our challenge, then, is to choose daily whether we will operate as a servant or stop and say, "Father, I am your child, and I choose to live and feel like your child." When we choose sonship, the miracle of grace becomes actualized in our heart the way God intended. This grace is his gift to us without any regard to our worthiness. Grace is the too-good-to-be-true good news!

The Joy and Grief of Discovering Grace

Lois, a forty-five-year-old woman, had been a Christian for over twenty years. She came to us struggling with depression and a terrible self-image. When she experienced conflict, particularly with her husband, she blamed herself. Sometimes she would physically hurt herself out of self-directed hatred and anger.

A committed Christian for most of her adult life, Lois participated in Bible study groups and attended conferences on personal healing and on growing in intimacy with God. To the best of her ability, she put God first in her life.

Yet through all her years of following God, Lois had a fundamental problem: she didn't know the true heart of the Father and the grace he offers. Of course she knew that it was only by grace that she had been saved, not by her own effort (Ephesians 2:8). However, this truth existed primarily in her mind, not her heart. Besides, it seemed more applicable to a person just coming to Christ than to someone who had followed Christ for many years. Like countless other Christians, Lois didn't understand the real, too-good-to-be-true gospel, so of course she wasn't living it out.

But in the course of the work that the Father did with Lois, she experienced a heart revelation of his grace. And that's when everything began to change.

Lois's journey into grace wasn't simple. She first had to see the core lies that misaligned her heart and behaviors from God's heart. She had to call upon his grace to touch childhood wounds that had significantly contributed to her distorted image of God, the gospel, and herself. Lois had to grieve. She had to forgive. She had to begin the process of embracing truth and rejecting lies, and she had to deal with destructive, toxic shame.

But as she partnered with God and walked with him into these places, he began to unfold his true beauty to her as well as allow her to see how beautiful she was to him.

There is a good, actually wonderful, part of Lois's story of finding grace. But there is a sad part as well. The good part is the freedom that Lois is beginning to experience in her relationship with God. Her intimacy with him now is tremendous compared to the past. The bad part is that she has lived the bulk of her Christian experience without this freedom and intimacy.

Although Lois is elated with her new relationship as a grace-filled follower of Christ, she still has had to grieve the loss of living so many years without this freedom. She has also begun to experience the Father's grief over his many children who do not truly know his heart. For many Christians—sold-out-for-God Christians, including leaders—live as Lois once did.

You Are Faithful

I (Jerry) so wish that I had internalized this message of grace earlier in my Christian walk. Yet I know that everything I have experienced, including the most difficult parts of my journey, have been and will continue to be used by God.

Thinking back on the times when I struggled with self-hatred and feeling terribly inadequate, I clearly recall how the Father *never* agreed with me. When I received individual prayer ministry at conferences, I heard the same message spoken over me again and again: "God calls you faithful."

Coming from so many different people, those words invariably induced the same emotional response: *busted!* Issued from the Father's unfathomable love and grace-filled heart, the prophecies directly hit the core of my shame and lies. It was here that the warfare existed and the battle would ultimately be won.

And I should not have been surprised that Jesus would call me faithful. Often in the Bible, he called his followers by names that didn't seem to fit. For instance, he called Peter "The Rock" at a time when Peter was anything but strong and stable. Jesus knows our hearts, and he defines us by what he sees and knows—and not by anything else.

Pleasing God Versus Trusting God

In an excellent book titled *The Cure: What If God Isn't Who You Think He Is and Neither Are You*,[40] the authors identify two roads that represent two very different ways of living. One is marked "Pleasing God;" the other, "Trusting God." You must choose which path you will travel.

Let's say that you decide to take the road that leads to "Pleasing God," expecting that if you travel down it, you will ultimately end up in a place where God is satisfied with you. As you walk down this path, you come to a room, and on its door is a sign that says, "Striving to Be All God Wants Me to Be." Turning a door knob labeled "Self-effort," you open the door and enter the "Room of Good Intentions."

Doesn't that seem like the destination you want? You long to please God. He is certainly worthy of pursuing him in this manner. So "Pleasing God" must be the road you want to travel—right?

But if pleasing God is your primary motive, you will ultimately find yourself working on sinning less and being good more in order to achieve an intimate relationship with God. And if you haven't realized it yet, when you try to sin less, you sin more! Moreover, when you try to be good and do good things for God, there is always more good to do. Traveling the "Pleasing God" road will wrap you up in performance. You'll learn to wear a mask. And in the process of performing and mask-wearing, you'll grow increasingly tired. But you won't dare admit it, because the "Room of Good Intentions" is not a safe place to express weakness and vulnerability. In this room, your relationship with God depends on your ability and strength.

Pleasing God without Trusting God

Is it possible to please God but not really trust him? You can certainly try. Have you ever wanted to do well for a boss and please him with your performance? Was it because of how much you trusted in him, knowing that he had your best interests at heart? Maybe. But you also sensed that if you didn't please him, you would suffer some type of negative consequence. So the real reason for your actions might have been rooted in a fear of your boss.

Let's say, though, that you didn't fear your boss's power over you. What you really needed was his approval and his affirmation. What would your motivation be in this situation? How would you know when your best was enough?

Let's apply this principle to your relationship with God. And let's assume that your heart truly desires to serve and please God. How do you know when he is pleased with you? Does he go by how many times you've read your Bible or prayed that day or week? How much you gave to the poor or served at your church? How well you have avoided sinful thoughts, words, or actions? What criteria do you use, and what is the standard you seek to achieve?

And what if you somehow determine that all your efforts are indeed pleasing God? Does that mean you trust him? Based on our example of pleasing the boss, the answer obviously is no.

Trusting God Pleases God

We like how Hebrews 11:6 reads in *The Message*:

It's impossible to please God apart from faith. And why? Because anyone who wants to approach God must believe both that he exists *and* that he cares enough to respond to those who seek him.

The Greek word used here for *faith—pistis—*would be better translated as *trust*. Therefore, it's impossible to please God without trusting God.

And if you trust God, you believe that he exists and that he is who he says he is. You also believe that he cares enough to respond to those who seek him—that he is trustworthy. You no longer base your actions on who you are and what you can do, but instead on who God is and what he can do.

A Place of Grace

As the authors of *The Cure* describe, another path with a different room is available.[41] It is the path of "Trusting God," and it leads into the "Room of Grace." Here, the sign on the door says, "Living Out of Who God Says I Am" and the door knob is "Humility." Stepping through the door, you enter a place where your relationship with God depends not on your ability to do good or not do bad, but rather on your trust in God and the work he is doing in you. In the "Room of Grace," you find yourself standing right next to God with his arm always around you. Your sins and struggles lie in front of you, and together you view them and work on them.

In this "Room of Grace" there is no pretense, no need to wear masks. You are free to be your authentic self; you and others in the room with you can acknowledge your common weaknesses and vulnerabilities. Grace, the enabling power of God, can do its work.

On the "Trusting God" path, you can truly please God and mature in your faith. While you may find yourself doing some of the same things you did on the "Pleasing God" path, now your actions originate from a very different place in your heart—from a place of grace.

Grace and the Recovery of Our Childhood

In his book *Shame and Grace*, Lewis Smedes shares that the healing of our shame begins with a spiritual experience of grace:

> To experience grace is to recover our lost inner child. The heart of our inner child is trust. We lose our childhood when we feel that the persons we trusted to accept us do not accept us or that they may reject us if we do things that displease them. Shame cheats us of childhood. Grace gives it back to us.
>
> The trusting child does not have a worry in the world about whether he is smart enough, or handsome enough, whether he has accomplished enough with his life, or been good enough to be acceptable to his parent[s]. He trusts that the someone who holds him, warms him, feeds him, cradles him, and loves him will accept him again and always. Trust is the inner child we rediscover in an experience of grace.
>
> Grace overcomes shame, not by uncovering an overlooked cache of excellence in ourselves but simply by accepting us, the whole of us, with no regard to our beauty or our ugliness, our virtue or our vices. We are accepted wholesale. Accepted with no possibility of being rejected. Accepted once and accepted forever. Accepted at the ultimate depth of our being. We are given what we have longed for in every nook and nuance of every relationship.[42]

Receiving and Giving Away the Good News

When did the "good news" stop being the too-good-to-be-true good news, the beyond-anything-we-could-hope-or-imagine good news, the amazing-awesome-unbelievable good news, the jump-up-and-down-and-spin-around-rejoicing good news? Has it *ever* been this for you?

Take the subject of tithing, for instance. When was the last time a sermon on giving felt good? A friend of mine shared a funny vignette from her church. The pastor had invited the little children to come to the front, sit down, and listen to a story. In telling it, he told the kids to imagine Jesus walking in with a delicious chocolate pie. "All I ask," Jesus said, "is that you give me one piece of the pie and you can have the other nine pieces." Immediately, a little boy in the front yelled out, "That's a good deal!" In the big, wide eyes of a child, that is good news!

One of our clients had come for ministry and had received more healing and a deeper heart-connection with the grace of God. Shortly after, she sent us the following letter:

> Since my time with you, I've made a new friend. She is struggling in her marriage—in some of the ways my husband and I have struggled. She feels like she made a mistake getting married and now she is paying for it—like God is punishing her. It is so clear to me how much God loves her and how his heart is broken for her as she experiences these circumstances. It's also clear to me that he is crazy about her and she is s-o-o-o NOT in trouble with him. The Father allows us to experience the consequences of our actions (he walks with us through this), but it's not a "punishment." We're not "in trouble." I have been able to share all these things with my new friend because that is what I've learned about him and his heart. That is what he showed me. I love it!

We believe that stories like these embody how the gospel will once again become good news—the too-good-to-be-true good news to God's children. It is the kind of news that gives life to the giver and hope to the receiver. We become the living messages of our Father's love.

Brennan Manning, in his classic book *The Ragamuffin Gospel*, says this about grace:

> Because salvation is by grace through faith, I believe that among the countless number of people standing in front of the throne and in front of the Lamb, dressed in white robes and holding palms in their hands (Revelation 7:9), I shall see the prostitute

from the Kit-Kat Ranch in Carson City, Nevada, who tearfully told me she could find no other employment to support her two-year-old son. I shall see the woman who had an abortion and is haunted by guilt and remorse but did the best she could faced with grueling alternatives; the businessman besieged with debt who sold his integrity in a series of desperate transactions; the insecure clergyman addicted to being liked, who never challenged his people from the pulpit and longed for unconditional love; the sexually-abused teen molested by his father and now selling his body on the street, who, as he falls asleep each night after his last 'trick', whispers the name of the unknown God he learned about in Sunday school; the death-bed convert who for decades had his cake and ate it, broke every law of God and man, wallowed in lust and raped the earth.

"But how?" we ask. Then the voice says, "They have washed their robes and made them white in the blood of the Lamb."

There they are. There *we* are—the multitude who so wanted to be faithful, who at times got defeated, soiled by life, and bested by trials, wearing the bloodied garments of life's tribulations, but through it all clung to the faith.

My friends, if this is not good news to you, you have never understood the gospel of grace.[43]

A Concluding Testimony: Resting in God's Love and Grace

Dear J and D,

I am writing to share with you what has transpired since my counseling time with you earlier this month. I can honestly say that I have never walked in more freedom than this before. It is almost awkward. I have not read my Bible all week, but have focused on the "Father's Love Letter" you gave me and on the subject of grace. I feel so much of his love and I don't have to strive anymore. At first, I had a fearful thought, "What if I never have a desire to read my Bible again?" But, as the days have gone by, I know that is not true. I have more of a passion and desire for God than I have ever had before, but I am able to rest, to sit with him and to let his love wash over me.

I don't feel like I have to perform all of these religious deeds to be a "Good Christian" but I can just be. I am confident that there will be a day soon that these religious traditions will become intimate places with the Lord where I don't have to strive anymore. I can see the day when I will read my Bible not to "be good" or to "be disciplined" but because I am resting in the love and grace of God.

There truly has been a shift on the inside of me, one that is hard to put into words. I think John Lynch puts it so well when he defines one path as "Trusting God" and the other as "Pleasing God." Without knowing it, I have been trying to please God with my greatest efforts, but not trusting him. I am now feeling so affirmed in who I am as a daughter of God.

Blessings,
Madeline

When I (Denise) was a little girl, I would go with my family to the Fourth of July fireworks. Lying on our blankets on the grass or sitting on our folding chairs on the bank of the Saginaw River, we got a spectacular view. Some people sat on the hoods of their cars, and when a round of fireworks earned *ooohs!* and *aaahhhhs!* from the crowd, the car horns would start sounding. Since we were not in a car, we would just say, "Honk, honk!"

That's how I feel reading the above letter. *Wow,* God! Honk, honk!

P R A Y E R

Father, I am grateful for the work of Jesus in my life. Although I was once lost in my sinful nature, yet because of my faith in you, I am now your beloved child and a new creation. Yet I still struggle to grasp this reality. I struggle with believing that you see me as righteous and with seeing myself in that truth.

Father, when I reject this truth in the deepest place, I reject the completed work of your Son. I don't want that. Lord, I declare that when you look upon me you see me as your righteous child. Therefore I, too, declare that I am righteous—a saint, a holy one set apart by you and for you.

Lord, I want to fulfill the destiny and calling that you have placed within me. I want to fly, not crawl. I want to be transformed into more of your likeness and into the fullness of whom you created me to be. But Lord, I know that I cannot do this on my own. I submit my heart to you and I invite you to reveal, heal, and lead me in this transforming work. I choose to trust you, for you are a good Father who desires the best for me. Please continue to take these truths into the deepest places of my heart, and give me the grace—your enabling power—to see, love, and accept myself, and then others, the way you do. In Jesus's name, amen.

QUESTIONS FOR REFLECTION

1. How have the shoulds and oughts of pleasing and performing affected the message of grace you extend to yourself? (A good clue is in how hard you are on yourself.)

2. Throughout the New Testament, the followers of Christ were referred to as *saints*—that is, *set-apart ones*. If you are a Christ-follower today, have you been able to see yourself as a saint? Why or why not?

3. Given two choices—the path of "Pleasing God and Striving to Be All God Wants Me to Be" or the path of "Trusting God and Living out of Who God Says I Am"—which one do you choose? Has this changed for you?

4. Describe the too-good-to-be-true good news of grace as presented in this chapter. Can you feel how loving and freeing this message of God's grace is meant to be? Explain.

5. Reread the closing prayer and ask yourself what you believe. In areas where you struggle, ask the Lord to help your unbelief.

CHAPTER ELEVEN

BE GOOD TO YOU + BE GOD TO YOU = LOVING WHO GOD LOVES

Your life and my life are, each of them, one of a kind. No one has lived your life or my life before, and no one will ever live them again. Our lives are unique stones in the mosaic of human existence—priceless and irreplaceable.
—Henri Nouwen

Love God. Love Self. Love Others.

We have now come full circle back to the premise of this book: the missing commandment—loving what God loves. We must love ourselves and like ourselves just as much as God loves us and really likes us. And then we must turn around and love others the same way.

Jesus said, "'Love the Lord your God with all your passion and prayer and intelligence.' This is the most important [of God's commandments], the first on any list. But there is a second to set alongside it: 'Love others as well as you love yourself.' These two commands are pegs; *everything* in God's Law and the Prophets hangs from them" (Matthew 22:37–40 MSG, emphasis added).

I can begin to love myself by being gentle to myself, being grace-filled toward myself, being responsible, caring, and attentive to myself. In this way, I can grow and discover who I am, which is who God says I am. From this place of identity, the Father will unveil my destiny, the plans he has for me. As this transformation takes place, there will be a new set of freedoms that will begin to evolve within my spirit—where I can begin to discover:

I am free to make choices that bring me life beyond mere survival.

I am free to have my own values and way of doing things.

I am free to make decisions that honor my own priorities.

I am free to respect myself enough to say no when that is best for me.

I am free to make mistakes and not be perfect.

I am free to relax and rest without feeling that I have to be busy to approve of myself.

I am free to forgive myself and not hold any part of myself in contempt.

I am free to feel my emotions, work through my emotions, and not shame my emotions.

I am free from being responsible for the feelings of others.

I am free from being a fixer, a savior, or a peacekeeper.

I am free to embrace change and growth within me.

I am free to love myself and receive love because I have value and worth.

I am free to be *fully me*.

Marsha's Story: Discovering the Power of God's Unearned Love

Dear J and D,

I am feeling so affirmed in who I am as a daughter of God. I had a unique moment as I sat in class the day after I got back from my ministry time with you. My professor, so full of life and love, was talking about sharing with his children their significance in the eyes of God. He was describing that they are home-schooled and that they struggle with mathematics. He told the class, "Whenever my children are struggling with a subject in school I say to them tenderly, 'How many math problems do you have to get right for Jesus to love you?—NONE! You are loved by God and are significant to him, not because of what you do but because you were made by him, and he just loves you because you are YOU!'"

My eyes filled with tears as my teacher spoke to us. It felt like he was speaking to me as his child. I was able to receive something then that I never experienced with my own father. It was a powerful, powerful moment for me. In that moment, it was almost as if my teacher was a surrogate father and I felt like I was receiving his message when I was 8 years old. For the first time in my life, I felt in my HEART—not just in my head—that I was significant to God. For so long I have KNOWN this truth, but have not FELT this truth.

The Lord is also beginning to undo a pattern of people pleasing and burden bearing in my life. I have begun to understand that I take on the burdens of others—ones that I am not supposed to carry. I know that the Lord has much more to reveal to me in this area, but I feel as if I have been set on the right path. I am excited for the journey ahead as I continue to walk in freedom and to grow in my identity in Christ.

Blessings to you,
Marsha

I Am the Father's Love

Several years ago, at a deliverance conference in Colorado, I (Denise) responded to a call for prayer. I was experiencing a lot of depression in my life at the time, and I wanted to hear something personal from the Father to me.

As the speaker moved through the crowd, he touched each person and spoke a word of blessing. "More, Lord." "Bless her, Lord." Over and over I heard the man pray the same words. But when he got to me, he said something different. His words were, simply, "The Father's love." It was a God thing. I heard the speaker bless over 500 people individually, and he never said "The Father's love" again.

Now, I could have interpreted this phrase to mean that God wanted me to focus on his love. But I heard a different meaning in my heart. I took those words as my name, my identity: I am "The Father's love." When God looks at me, he calls me his love. I am the object of his love.

I am the Father's love! And that is just one of many important "I am" truths. Others include:

I am God's delight.
I am the one Jesus loves.
I am his beloved.
I am his pearl of great price.
I am a jewel in his crown.
I am me—and I'm okay.

A Story of Walking Free

After we meet with clients, we ask them to provide us with an update of the impact of the counseling experience. This client chose to share, in a story format, what he learned:

My parents had the appearance of being good parents, but little emotional intimacy was expressed in my home growing up. My father was unable to show me direct love or affection. At twenty-five years of age, I found myself without much of an identity and having a difficult time relating to Father God.

I stuffed down the pain of my childhood and adolescence and began to hate myself, never realizing that my difficulty in making decisions, my lack of direction, my lack of identity, and my fear and anxiety all resulted directly from a loss in my childhood. I believed the lie that my lack in those areas was because I was a terrible person. I hated myself. But the real problem wasn't me—it was a wound. The areas I hated in myself were directly related to the wounding I had received early in life.

Once I understood my father wound, I began to realize how much shame I had carried like a weight for so many years. I have recognized that I am in desperate need of a Father who will console his son when he is hurting and sad. Today I find myself sometimes going into a room with my heavenly Father and just letting him hold me and comfort me like he has wanted to do for so long. I am ever so close to fully embracing that I am a son of God. The shame I have carried around has kept me from intimacy with him.

I have learned that my striving is a mask. All my life I have strived to please God instead of trusting him. But now I choose to trust that I am who the Scriptures say I am: a new creation with a new nature—a good heart that seeks after God and longs for him. I want to live in the room of grace and let the Father love on me.

God wants me to be real in my life, and he is healing my heart and leading me to be the man he created me to be. Trusting him in this process is more sincere than striving for some type of perfection which I will only use as a standard for judging myself.

I see now the importance of grieving my losses and no longer excusing my parents; yet I also know that I can forgive my parents. I also recognize my need to understand my shame and to know the difference between healthy and unhealthy shame so that I can discern my Father's voice and actions towards me.

Today, I make a practice of looking at myself in the mirror and encouraging myself. Instead of trying to do right and be something, I am trusting and seeking the Lord. I am wrapping my arms around the truth that, like Jesus, I am my Father's son, in whom he is well-pleased.

I feel that the more I can lean into the Father and receive his love, the more I will be able to move on and truly live for him. Living in the room of grace prepares me for the destiny he wants to launch me into. The Father wants me to trust in him and let him comfort my pain.

These days, I become teary-eyed much more often as I experience more emotions. I know that the floodgates of my tears will open soon—and that is good. I feel that I can face the future, and know I will walk free of my pain and be able to love those around me with a fatherly love—the same love that my heavenly Father feels toward me.

Soon we will all be ready to tell our healing story—when the story of our past no longer controls us. When it is no longer stuffed down inside us, buried alive. In the healing journey, we learn what happened to us, we realize that it mattered, and we find out where we go next.

We discover what is meaningful. Grievous. Painful.

We risk. We share. We interact. We discover. We grow.

We heal.

We heal because we are the child of the One who came to heal the brokenhearted. We are free to *be*come, and to come to *be*, all that he created us to *be*. We are uniquely knit by a heavenly Father who is quite pleased with *everything* he makes. Reread Genesis 1 MSG if you want to check on this. Its grand conclusion is verse 31: "God looked over everything he had made; it was so good, so very good!"

Becoming a Child at Play

A writer friend of ours shared with us a story she wrote. We offer it here because it captures something: the wonder, the awe, the infectious power of a child at play. It seems like the Father wants this child to be you—YOU.

See if you agree.

I went to the Sautee General Store yesterday for a quick sandwich to go. Their BLT's are like a taste of summer. I got in my car in a hurry to be on my way. When I was buckling up, I saw a bubble float past my window. I looked toward the flower-bed, where the bubble solution is set upon a pedestal. Amid the dancing flowers was a dancing boy, four, maybe five years old. He carried the bubble wand in his hand like a scepter ... waving it as if he was king of the bubbles. The shine in his blue eyes was magical. It captured the attention of an older lady slowly making her way down the stairs of the store. She stopped mid-step to take in the sight of his blond hair bouncing around in summertime ecstasy. Her wrinkled cheeks climbed into a smile and the sparkle in her eyes matched his. For a moment, the years faded from her face. I wondered how far back in time she had been transported.

Others who were milling around, tourists mostly, stopped as well. All eyes were transfixed on the boy, who was oblivious to anything but creating the most bubbles possible. As we all watched him, his dad approached. He took the wand and, like dads do, began to make longer and bigger bubbles for the boy. If the boy had been a balloon at that moment, he would have burst. He ran, chasing the bubbles. Catching them. Popping them. He laughed and giggled. I know because I rolled down my window to hear. His dad was cheering him on. The boy caught up in a moment of childhood we all remember. The smile on his little sun-burned face had spread to the faces of the twelve or so people frozen in place around him. Each of us waiting for the spell to be broken, but hoping it wouldn't just yet. The simplicity of the moment struck me ... how a bit of soapy water and a wire could transform a scene of strangers into time traveling playmates. How a little boy could inject life in a brief instant to all those around him, yet not even know it.

I think that God loves for us to play as children. When we dance and are thrilled at his creation, he cheers us on. When we rejoice in the simplest little things ... like bubbles and raindrops, fire-flies and rainbows ... it blesses him. When we are infused with joyful exuberance, time stands still. He longs to be with us when we are in such a state. It is simple, this communion with him. No words are needed. The music of our laughter, the abandon of our hearts to the moment, it is like no other time. We remember it from childhood but we need to be reminded. Our memories refreshed. What is this old familiar feeling that rises up at the sight of a child at play? It is freedom. It is unhindered innocence. It is honesty. It is worship.[44]

A Poem for Reflection

As we close this chapter, we would like to share a hope-giving poem about the five stages in the journey of healing. May it be a guide for your progress.

Portrait of Progress

> I. I walk down the street.
>> There is a deep hole in the sidewalk.
>>> I fall in.
>>>> I am lost … I am helpless.
>>>> It isn't my fault.
>>>> It takes forever to find a way out.

> II. I walk down the same street.
>> There is a deep hole in the sidewalk.
>>> I pretend I don't see it.
>>> I fall in again.
>>>> I can't believe I'm in the same place,
>>>> But, it isn't my fault.
>>>> It still takes a long time to get out.

> III. I walk down the same street.
>> There is a deep hole in the sidewalk.
>>> I see it there.

I still fall in … it's a habit.

My eyes are open.

I see where I am.

It's my fault.

I get out immediately.

IV. I walk down the same street.

There is a deep hole in the sidewalk.

I walk around it.

V. I walk down another street.[45]

PRAYER

Father, thank you for your process of redemption and restoration—big words that have a simple meaning: that I am important enough to you that you made a way to find me, heal my heart, and bring me to a new place. Thank you that you sent your Son, Jesus, to heal my broken heart and set me free from the things that have kept me bound in some way. Your Word says that "it is for freedom that Christ has set us free." I stand in that freedom and I refuse to accept anything less.

I know that I am unable to do anything without your help, including living from a place of freedom and life, so I ask you for your help to continue to love and accept myself and live from your heart. Help me to love you, myself, and others in the way you intended. In Jesus's name, amen.

QUESTIONS FOR REFLECTION

1. As a brief but powerful exercise, look at yourself in the mirror and say, "I am the Father's love." Commit this message to memory and choose to live it out. It will bless you and God.

2. What does this statement mean for you: "The Father wants you to be free to *become*, and to come to *be*, all that he created you to *be*."

3. Go back to the section "Becoming a Child at Play." Imagine that you are one of the tourists. What do you *feel* as you watch this child? Stop and imagine yourself as being this child at play. How do you think the Father feels as he watches? Can you imagine that he also delights over you and enjoys you?

4. Referring to the "Portrait of Progress" as a map, where do you find yourself on the healing journey? Use the "Portrait of Progress" as a guidebook until you find yourself walking down another street.

5. Pray the closing prayer for yourself. We join our prayer with yours for the fullness of love and life!

EPILOGUE

To Our Readers: Thank You

We are blessed you have come with us on this healing path. It is a journey that is worth the trouble and worth the risk. In closing, we wish to share with you one more time a basic yet profound truth: God is with you. Throughout your journey to healing and wholeness and life, be assured of this:

> God is here. Right now. On your side. At your side. His arm is around you. He is actively seeking to help you and will never, *ever* leave you. He is looking with you at your struggles, your questions, your wrestlings. It is you and him together. He is an ever-present help in trouble. He is passionate about YOU—the delight and pride of his life.

> This is good news. *Incredibly* good news. This, dear friends, is the true gospel.

> But for right now … we have three things to do … Trust steadily in God, hope unswervingly, love extravagantly. And the best of the three is love. (1 Corinthians 13:13 MSG)

SOURCES

Endnotes

1 Beth Moore, *Breaking Free* (Nashville: Broadman and Holman, 2000), 197.

2 John Eldredge, *Waking the Dead* (Nashville: Thomas Nelson, 2003), 211-212.

3 Alfred Ells, *One-Way Relationships Workbook* (Nashville: Thomas Nelson, 1992), 13.

4 Henri Nouwen, *The Inner Voice of Love* (New York: Doubleday, 1996) 78-79.

5 Mike Mason, *The Mystery of Children* (Colorado Springs: WaterBrook Press, 2001) 176-177.

6 John Eldredge, *The Way of the Wild Heart* (Nashville: Thomas Nelson, 2006).

7 For a detailed account of her story, see http://www.passionate healthonline.com/letter_teresa.html.

8 Donald Miller, *Father Fiction*, (New York: Howard Books, 2010), 38-39.

9 For more information see http://www.fathersloveletter.com/text.html.

10 Mike Bickle, *The Pleasures of Loving God*, (Lake Mary, FL: Creation House, 2000), 68-69.

11 James Bryan Smith, *The Good and Beautiful God*, (Downers Grove, IL: Intervarsity Press, 2009), 121.

12 Abraham Joshua Heschel, *God in Search of Man*, (New York: The Noonday Press, 1983), 74.

13 S. J. Hill, *Enjoying God*, (Lake Mary, FL: Relevant Media Group, 2001), 90–91.

14 Miller, *Father Fiction*, 47.

15 Ibid. 49-50.

16 Julianne Maki and Mark Maki, *Christian Adults in Recovery* (Brea, CA: self-published, 1992), 95–96.

17 David Stoop, *Making Peace with Your Father* (Wheaton, IL: Tyndale House, 2004), 150-151.

18 Miller, *Father Fiction*, 35-36.

19 Roland Warren, interview by Matt Lauer, *NBC Today Show*, June 11, 2010.

20 Miller, *Father Fiction*, 38.

21 Jack Frost, *Experiencing the Father's Embrace* (Lake Mary, FL: Charisma House, 2002), 112–113.

22 Henri Nouwen, *Life of the Beloved* (New York: Crossroad Books, 1992), 93–95, 100–101.

23 John Eldredge, *Wild at Heart* (Nashville: Thomas Nelson, 2001), 128–129.

24 John and Paula Sandford, *The Transformation of the Inner Man* (Tulsa: Victory House, Inc., 1982), 191-205.

25 Maki and Maki, *Christian Adults in Recovery*, vii.

26 Judy Emerson, *In the Voice of a Child* (Nashville: Thomas Nelson, 1994), 71-72.

27 CharlesWhitfield, MD, *Healing the Child Within* (Deerfield Beach, FL: Health Communications, Inc., 1989), 46–47.

28 Chester and Betsy Kylstra, *An Integrated Approach to Healing Ministry* (Kent, England: Sovereign World, 2003), 130–133.

29 John Bradshaw, *Homecoming* (New York: Bantam Books, 1990), 47–49.

30 Elizabeth Kubler-Ross, *On Death and Dying* (New York: Scribner, 1969), 263-264.

31 Neil Anderson, *Ministering the Steps to Freedom in Christ* (Delight, AR: Gospel Light, 1998), 54-56.

32 Brennan Manning, *The Signature of Jesus* (Sisters, OR: Multnomah, 1996), 100-101.

33 R.T. Kendall, *Total Forgiveness* (Lake Mary, FL: Charisma House, 2002), 162.

34 James Bryan Smith, *Embracing the Love of God* (San Francisco: Harper, 1995), 37–38.

35 St. Bernard of Clairvaux, *On Loving God*, quoted in John Eldredge, *Waking the Dead* (Nashville: Nelson Books, 2003), 213.

36 *Nelson's Illustrated Bible Dictionary* (Nashville: Thomas Nelson, 1986), PC Study Bible, V4.1A.

37 *Vine's Expository Dictionary of Biblical Words* (Nashville: Thomas Nelson, 2000), PC Study Bible, V4.1A.

38 James Bryan Smith, *The Good and Beautiful God* (Downer's Grove, IL: InterVarsity Press, 2009), 155–156.

39 David Seamands, *Healing Grace* (Wheaton, IL: Victor Books, 1988), 23–24.

40 John Lynch, Bruce McNicol, and Bill Thrall, *The Cure: What If God Isn't Who You Think He Is And Neither Are You* (San Clemente, CA: CrossSection, 2011), 27–38.

41 Ibid.

42 Lewis Smedes, *Shame and Grace* (San Francisco: Harper, 1993), 108–109.

43 Brennan Manning, *The Ragamuffin Gospel*, (Sisters, OR: Multnomah, 1990), 29.

44 Michelle Gunnin, "Child at Play." http://www.mgunnin.blog.com. July 31, 2010.

45 Portia Nelson, *Portrait of Progress*, quoted in Maki and Maki, Christian Adults in Recovery, 105.

ACKNOWLEDGMENTS

First to God our Father: Thank you, Father, for giving us a glimpse of your tangible yet unfathomable heart for us and for inspiring us to write this book. Thank you for bringing your treasures—your children—to The Father's Heart Intensive Christian Counseling Ministry and trusting us with their pain and broken hearts. We are honored and humbled by your trust in us. We are awestruck by the ways you have orchestrated a connection between us and people from across the United States and around the globe.

To our clients: Thank you for trusting us with your broken hearts and lives. Your stories have touched us and pierced us deeply. You have enriched us with a facet of the Father's heart that we would never have seen without you allowing us to be a part of your healing journey and your life story. You are never forgotten.

To our (Denise's) sister Gloria: You were the first one to read (more than once) and critique our book. Thank you for all of your valuable suggestions and your words of heart-felt encouragement. Our favorite was your email that said—"I have read through page 10, and I am already crying … again! I LOVE THIS BOOK!" These words mean more than you can imagine. We love you, sis.

To our board members, our intercessors, our friends, our families: Thank you for your love, your prayers, and your ongoing encouragement. You make a difference!—and we are so grateful for your hearts for us and for this ministry.

To publisher Kevin Miles of Heart & Life Publishers and editor Bob Hartig: What a God-connection this has been! You are exactly the type of people that we wanted to be involved in this project. We look forward to what God has planned as we continue to work together.